WHEN A MAN LOVES A WOMAN

CLAUDE
M.
STEINER

WHEN A MAN LOVES A WOMAN

SEXUAL AND
EMOTIONAL LITERACY
FOR THE
MODERN MAN

GROVE PRESS, INC., NEW YORK

Excerpts from The Hite Report on Male Sexuality by Shere Hite
(Copyright © 1981 by Shere Hite) reprinted by permission of
Alfred A. Knopf, Inc.

Excerpts from The Hite Report: A Nationwide Study of
Female Sexuality by Shere Hite (Copyright © 1976 by Shere
Hite) reprinted by permission of Macmillan Publishing Company.

First Grove Press Edition 1986
First Printing 1986
ISBN: 0-394-54945-7
Library of Congress Catalog Card Number: 85-71164

First Evergreen Edition 1986
First Printing 1986
ISBN: 0-394-62076-3
Library of Congress Catalog Card Number: 85-71164

Library of Congress Cataloging in Publication Data
Steiner, Claude, 1935–
    When a man loves a woman.
    1. Interpersonal relations.   2. Intimacy (Psychology)
3. Sex (Psychology)   4. Women—United States—Attitudes.
I. Title.
HM132.S68   1986   306.7   85-71164
ISBN 0-394-54945-7
ISBN 0-394-62076-3 (pbk.)

Designed by Abe Lerner
Printed in the United States of America
Grove Press, Inc., 196 West Houston Street, New York, N.Y. 10014

                              1   3   5   4   2

TO MY SON, ERIC

MY BROTHER, MIGUEL

MY FATHER, WILLY

AND LAST BUT NOT LEAST

TO MYSELF AND ALL MY BROTHERS.

CONTENTS

ACKNOWLEDGMENTS

Though I had always wanted to write a book for men on the subject of love and sex I never took that wish seriously until Fred Jordan suggested that I write a response to Alexandra Penny's bestseller *How to Make Love to a Man*. I had written a series of papers and pamphlets (*Letter to a Brother* and *Feminism for Men*) concerning issues that the women's movement had brought into men's lives. But my first reaction to the notion that I would attempt such a book was that it was a presumptuous undertaking sure to make me the target of criticism and scorn from men and women alike.

"Who was I," I asked, "to write about such matters?" To my surprise both male and female friends and colleagues encouraged me to go ahead. After considerable soul searching I plunged into the work that was to have been completed within one year.

A few weeks after I signed the contract with Fred Jordan Books, Michael Morgenstern announced the publication of his book *How to Make Love to a Woman*. Alexandra Penny having been answered, I relaxed; five years and ten drafts later, with the help of scores of friends, the project is complete. I am very glad to have had the chance to expend time and careful thought on this book; it has been as much of an educational experience for me as I hope it will be for my readers. When I started to write the book, I was armed with a number of important and worthwhile notions about men and women and a great deal of sympathy for women's quandaries. I emerged from the project with a much improved attitude toward men and sympathy for the difficulties that face them in the proverbial war of the sexes.

The book I wrote, however, was not the book Fred Jordan had envisioned, and for three long years I had no publisher. I am thankful for having had that period of time in which to improve the book. Eventually, it caught Barney Rosset's eye, and I am happy to be again published by Grove Press. I thank Barney for his enthusiastic response and support for the book.

The research upon which this book is based is threefold: First, hundreds of women in the U.S., Latin America, and Europe were questioned by myself and a team of women interviewers. There was no attempt to gather this data in a scientifically rigorous manner; the questionnaire was only intended to provide a look at a wide variety of women and their attitudes about men. Thanks are due to Darca Nicholson, Jude La Barre, and Sandy Spiker for their help designing and administering the questionnaire.

The second source of information was research done by others, especially Shere Hite's studies of male and female sexuality.

Finally, I based the book on my own experience plus information gathered over a period of twenty years of practice as a clinical psychologist and mediator.

Thanks are due also to Bruce Carroll, Terry Cannon, Jo Ann Costello, Norman de Vall, Deirdre English, David Geisinger, Frances Hayward, Tom Hine, Becky Jenkins, Jaime Kanton, Charles Rappleye, Gail Rebuck, Beth Roy, Harvey Tappin, my brother Miguel Steiner, and Mimi Steiner, my daughter, for their careful reading and valuable feedback.

Thanks to Jackson Browne for suggesting the name for this book and to Percy Sledge for bringing it to us in the first place.

Very special thanks to Fred Jordan for suggesting that I write this book and for his untiring support and invaluable feedback.

Susan Pepperwood and Caryn Levin typed and discussed thousands of pages of the early manuscript, and Diane Benedict provided typing and valuable comment for the final version.

My heartfelt thanks to the members of the Bay Area Radical Psychiatry Collective, Becky Jenkins, Beth Roy, Darca Nicholson, Shelby Morgan, Sandy Spiker, Jo Ann Costello, Barbara Moulton, Jude La Barre, Diana Rabenold and Mark Weston, who provided moral support, insight, personal problem solving, and feedback during the last five years.

Sandy Spiker, my editorial assistant, deserves special recognition for her contribution throughout; the design of the questionnaire, the interviews, the thorough editing of the book, and her faithful and intimate friendship. Her relentless but nurturing criticism of my work has been invaluable.

Thanks also to Darca Nicholson for being with me for many years of partnership and for adding Denali to my life. Darca was the source of many notions that found their way into the book.

Finally, I wish to thank Alan Rinzler for his brilliant editing job, which put the book in its final shape.

INTRODUCTION | THE NEW WOMEN:

ARE WE MEN

ENOUGH?

The events of the last thirty years have had a profound effect on people and their relationships. We have seen sexuality go through a major revolution. We have seen divorce become commonplace. Ordinary people are aware of the fact that they don't have to be trapped in destructive relationships, and both men and women are questioning the value of marriage. The "rule book" has been thrown out, and we find ourselves without clear guidelines as to how to proceed. Some say that those changes are threatening the very fiber of American society by causing the destruction of the family. Even those of us who welcomed these changes find ourselves wondering, "What now?"

It's clear that the gulf between men and women continues to be as large as or larger than it ever was. Women have changed: The woman of the 1980's is more powerful and self-sufficient; she wants to be treated as an equal at home and at work. She may want to have children, but may not want to be exclusively a homemaker. While she may want to be in a long-lasting relationship with a man, she is not afraid of being alone and is not willing to settle for a relationship that isn't satisfying or beneficial to her.

Today, such women are openly talking to each other and writing about their likes and dislikes. They are making legitimate, well-thought-out demands in the home, at work, and in bed. They want jobs with equal pay; they want wheels and muscles, and they want men to support their new independence and power. These women aren't interested in men who are going to fight them every step of the way in order to cling to outmoded styles of male domination.

Modern women are extremely challenging, if not alarming, to men. We want them by our sides, but are irritated by their claims. We love their energy, but fear that they're "ball breakers." We admire their self-reliance, but aren't quite sure we like their independence from us. To be with them makes us feel manly, but also challenges our manhood.

Men too have changed. They've changed in response to women's changes, but also on their own initiative. In the 1950's at the same time Betty Friedan launched the latest women's revolt with her book *The Feminine Mystique,* the appearance of *Playboy* magazine kicked off the "Playboy Philosophy." This philosophy (as Barbara Ehrenreich points out in *The Hearts of Men*) encouraged men to throw off their dreary male duties as breadwinners and heads of households and dared them to become playboys and spend their money on the good life as portrayed in the magazine's full-color ads.

Many men did just that. We avoided commitment to the traditional wife and family and went for the enormously attractive single life. We gave up the ranch house and the two-car garage and went instead for a town-house bachelor pad and a Porsche. Instead of saving our money for the kids' educations, we charged our skiing winters and tropical vacations on credit cards. Yet after experiencing our own liberation from domesticity, we are coming to agree in principle with women's wants. Men would, after all, prefer to live a harmonious life in a secure home filled with children and friends, with a woman they love, than be perennial bachelors—as long as life doesn't become a terminal velvet trap.

An entire generation of women and men deeply affected by the latest wave of feminism is coming of age. Even though many do not consider themselves even remotely feminist, these men and women could not live in the Tarzan-Jane, Ronald-Nancy mode if their survival depended on it.

We have come back to an old familiar position, but find ourselves on higher ground. Our interest in forming couples still remains. Coupling is a source of security, power, comfort, pleasure, and love. But couples have changed. In the past, couples were often based on two people who became one by each contributing half a person; he the brains and income, she the heart and nurturing. Today, couples are becoming partnerships of mutually respectful, loving equals working together to face life's hardships and enjoy its rewards.

These relationships are deeply affected by the liberating lessons of the 1960's and 1970's. In these relationships sexuality can be given full and lasting rein. Among these couples, binding love and commitment are expected to be mutual.

For men, marriage has traditionally been a terrifying decision. Many a groom has been dragged to the altar by his best man or propelled forward with a shotgun.

It has seemed to us, at times, that commitment to a woman is akin to a life sentence of forced labor, and in some cases this fear has come true. But the woman of the 1980's doesn't want a man for a slave any more than she wants him for a slave master. She wants a partner, and that is actually a new and desirable proposition for a man. Under these new circumstances, commitments can be totally different than they were twenty years ago. The burdens—both at home and in the workplace—are shared, and the rewards of the relationship—its pleasures, freedoms, and economic benefits—are shared equally as well. Commitment to a modern woman is beginning to look like a good deal.

Nevertheless, plenty of problems still remain between men and women. For one thing, men may have given up their old roles, but they are not sure of what their new roles are supposed to be. We're no longer sure how to treat women. All this liberation and equality have brought new expectations and burdens for us. In the eternal war of the sexes, many men feel that they have lost a battle; they feel martyred and put upon by all the changes that seem out of their control.

When a man loves a woman, he may have no idea how to proceed in a self-respecting and dignified manner. This book is meant for such men: for men who want to be comfortable friends and lovers with the women in their lives; for men who want to have long-lasting, secure, yet sexually plentiful, exciting relationships; and more importantly, for men who want to be loving, sexy and, dare I say, sweet. This book will tell you what today's women want from their friends, lovers, and mates, and how a man can become appreciated and sought after by today's woman.

CHAPTER 1

WHAT DO
WOMEN LIKE
ABOUT MEN?

During the last twenty years, what is admirable and likable about men has been obscured by the intense criticism stemming from the new perceptions and expectations of women. Therefore, I decided to find out what women *do* like about us. With the help of several associates, I asked hundreds of women the question "What do you like about men?" The answers often related to how he felt about himself:

"There is a certain way he uses himself, how he is open, at ease, comfortable, which attracts me about a man, even if he is not good-looking. It's an energy, a positive attitude. Not conceited or macho but comfortable with himself," said one woman in her thirties, a legal secretary for a large firm.

"I know some men think it's correct to be very self-critical and guilty about being a man, but to me it's a turnoff," said Patty, 29, a women's health social worker.

"I appreciate men who are willing to be questioned

about their sexism. But I don't like men who carry around a cloud of male guilt. It's a total wet blanket to my sexual feelings," was Dahlia's opinion. Dahlia is in her forties, recently divorced.

In spite of the heightened awareness women have developed about men's shortcomings, women, with a few exceptions, still like men and haven't given up on them.

"I like their bodies," another woman says. "I like their sturdiness, their solidity, how they are lean and hard. I like men who appreciate their own bodies. That's why I find gay men attractive. They are into the beauty of men's bodies and love their own. Gay men move so gracefully sometimes. The graceful male body is beautiful."

"I like men's penises. They are such a fantastic combination of strength and vulnerability. I like to cradle a man's testicles and penis in my hands when it's soft. The penis is such a fascinating gadget, the way it gets hard in your hand," said Mary.

"I really like the way men smell. With some men it was the most attractive, addictive thing. The way he starts to smell when we are making love. I did not want him to leave and take his smell with him," said Peggy, 36, a baker at a neighborhood bakery.

"I love men's forearms, upper arms, and shoulders. I find the muscles and veins, and their effective, powerful hands unbelievably sexy. I can look at a man's forearms and their shape turns me on. I have to look away," said Denise, a successful free-lance journalist.

Many women responded similarly. They liked men's muscle formation, their upper body strength, the density and firmness of male flesh, men's body hair, whis-

2

kers and baldness, their genitals, the timbre of their voices, and the way they smell.

Other women liked men's minds, the way they think. For instance, Janet, a psychiatric nurse, 23, said: "I like the way men understand machines and the way they can fix things. I like the way they approach a problem in a mechanical and systematic way, using logic and their minds as tools."

Another woman said, "Men are good at making you escape. C'mon, get your hat on, let's go! Women sit and stew. I like men's detachment skills, when they can also be close."

Tina, the mother of two small children, said, "I like the things in men that I, because I'm a woman, have been prevented from having. I like their capacity to stay cool; I like the way they can be high-strung, active, intense, humorous, aggressive. I like those things because they are things that are missing in me. I know I could do all those things too, but my upbringing led me away from them. So I like to get them from men."

"What do you like about men?" I asked Sandy, a carpenter in her early thirties.

"I like to work with men, they get the job done."

"That sounds like a sexist attitude. What do you mean?"

"They are more goal oriented. Women tend to have feelings at inappropriate times. I like to be able to plan with a man who works for me to do something by a certain time and get it done. With a woman I am liable to have to get into a discussion about feelings. With women often times I come up against the insidious psychology of how they were brought up, how their father treated them. I find it is very easy to push women's buttons. I might ask a woman to pass the hammer and that might be enough to trigger her to feel that she won't be able to deal with it. Men can take orders and do things efficiently."

"Men are so important," high school biology teacher Pilar, a Mexican woman of 32, assured me.

"How?" I asked.

"Not as bosses or soldiers, but as men, because they are men, and as men they have an important function in the scheme of things."

"What do you like about men?" I asked Rikki.

"I like men's tradition of courage and concern for people, their sense of responsibility. Men have much to be proud of in their history. There have been so many heroic men who have given their lives for important things. I admire that," she answered.

"What do you like about men?"

"I like their masculine tenderness—large and encompassing. I like the spark of their intelligence and open-heartedness. I like their capacity to protect me," answered Rocio, 23, a Spanish agronomy student.

After the question was asked many times, a pattern seemed to emerge: On one hand, women like men, as men, because of their genetic, physical characteristics of manhood. On the other hand, women like those characteristics that they themselves have been alienated from by the way men and women are brought up. Men are trained, generally, to be rational and unemotional, skilled with machines, assertive, willing to take up space. This desire to be with people who have what we lack is not particular to women. It's one large reason for men's need for women, who have the warmth and emotionality men often lack and long for.

The fact that this mutual attraction may be based on

4

a reciprocal shortcoming doesn't make it any less real or something to be ashamed of. For as long as women and men are different from each other, they'll look to each other to fulfill what they lack. Men can be proud of the things they are good at because they are men.

Our survey also revealed that women often liked in men the very things they complained about at other times. I had to ask myself, "Do women, when everything is said and done, really want men who are unemotional, aggressive, and mechanically inclined?" I was forced to reconsider the popular myth that women like to be dominated and protected by silent strong tall men. Apparently, this conception, which the women's movement has fought so hard, is not easily disposed of.

For example, Frances, 35, a highly paid editor living with a man and his and her children, said, "We [women] don't really know what we want. I like men to have feelings, but I don't want them to be angry. I want them to treat me as an equal, but I want them to be strong so I can lean on them. I resent their skills, but I still let them get their hands dirty while they fix my car." The ambiguity Frances expresses is not unusual; what *do* women want?

Eventually, I recognized the answer: Many of the qualities that are appreciated in men are also the things they are most disliked for—*when they are taken to an extreme*. As Karen, a woman in her forties who has known many men and given the matter much thought, said, "I *know* what I want. Strength without violence, feelings without sloppiness, skill without being patronized, logic without mind-rape. I want men to do what they do well in moderation and without expecting to be put on a pedestal for it."

Women clearly don't appreciate dominating, cold,

egotistical men. They also get no kick out of self-deprecating, guilty, withdrawn men. In other words, what women want is "no more macho, no more wimp."

Ultimately, and quite logically, what people like about men is what they also like about women—their humanness. They like their seriousness, their compassion and concern, their exuberance and good humor, their skill and intelligence, their healthy, strong bodies, their sexuality and joyfulness. They like being loved by them. They like being able to love them fully and without reservations.

Women like men's strength, virility, and boldness, and would like them to develop gentility, delicacy, and tenderness. And those are things that any man either has or can develop, provided he is truly interested in loving women.

CHAPTER 2 | WHAT DO
WOMEN DISLIKE
ABOUT MEN?

Having confirmed that there are, in fact, many things that women do like about men, I wanted to take a close look at those complaints about men that are voiced over and over by women, to see if there is some truth in them. So in our questionnaire, we also asked women what turned them off about men as friends and as lovers.

Many men are truly puzzled when certain complaints repeatedly come forward in their relationships at home, at work, or in conversations at gatherings. These complaints often seem out of context, practically out of the blue, and are frequently fueled with intense feeling, sometimes rage, which seems totally out of proportion to the facts of the matter. Some men can't understand any of it; some, only a small portion. Others understand the complaint, but can't deal with the heavy emotions and anger behind it. In these situations, some men will argue self-righteously or be extremely defensive; some will try to joke their way out, and some will dummy up.

I have frequently had the painful experience of witnessing a conversation in which a woman voiced an angry but legitimate complaint only to be faced with a man's summary invalidation of her point of view. The uselessness of these exchanges has struck me as saddening to the point of being tragic. The woman clearly had a point, but given the man's awareness, it was badly stated and mixed with so much feeling that only a man already acquainted with the complaint could weather the intense emotion. The usual male response of defensiveness serves only to reaffirm the woman's view, leaving a chilling gap between them. Consider the following drama overheard at a cocktail lounge.

Mary had been dancing with a man, and returned to her seat around a low table heaped with drinks. "What a creep!" she says.

"Extreme repulsivo, eh?" quips Sonja.

"Really, these guys think they are God's gift to women."

Reluctantly Frank takes the bait. "You didn't have to dance with him, you know."

"He wouldn't leave me alone. I thought I would get rid of him if I danced with him once."

"C'mon, you know you like it," Sam interrupts.

"What, having some slob rub himself all over me? What is it with you guys, you're so into getting laid that you can't tell when a woman isn't interested?"

"Oh, oh, here comes the woman's lip!"

"Listen, Sam, I'm no feminist, but I'm sick of horny guys who can't take no for an answer."

"If you can't stand the heat, stay out of bars, is what I say."

"Oh yeah? What gives you the right to tell me to stay out of bars? Next thing you are going to say is that I should stay out of the street and that if I get raped, I was asking for it!"

"Well, some streets, some nights, you would be asking for it."

"Yeah, and I suppose you are going to tell me that I'd enjoy it."

"I didn't say that, just that you've got to expect certain things in certain places!"

"Don't give me that, you really think I like being harassed by men..." (and so on).

In these familiar debates both the women and the men have a legitimate position: She resents the assumption that men's insistent pursuit is pleasing when, in fact, she felt intruded upon and wished to be left alone. He sincerely believes that in the context of a bar, men are correct to assume that she is available. Neither is responding to the other's point of view and the exchange produced more heat than light on the subject. Everyone around the table was left upset, and for some it spoiled the evening.

In this chapter I would like to clarify the woman's viewpoint with the hope of being helpful to my male readers.

It is reasonable to assume that most men are doing their best to be good men. Therefore, when we are lumped together as a group and accused of a typical male shortcoming ("All you want is sex—a typical male" or "Just like a man, emotionally retarded"), we need to realize that whether fair or not, these accusations are best *not* taken as personal attacks. If, in fact, we are unwittingly acting according to some primitive male tradition, then our behavior is the result of role training

9

for which we are not wholly to blame. As long as we don't understand what we are doing wrong, we cannot, in all fairness, be held responsible for it. We don't have to react with guilt and need not be defensive. Instead, we need to try to understand the criticism. And when we do, we can proceed to do something about it if we wish.

To help understand our male role behavior, it is useful to remember the following: When human beings are born, they are divided into two groups. One group is told: "When you grow up, you will be a girl, and you should be a supportive and nurturing person. In order to be truly good at being nurturing it will be useful for you to be intuitive and capable of reading people's minds, especially men's, because men, bless them, aren't good at asking for what they need. Since your major task will be to nurture, you won't need to be very rational. You don't need rationality in order to be supportive; in fact, rationality interferes and could even be detrimental to nurturing. It is best to try not to understand certain things."

The other group is told: "When you grow up, you will be a man. A good man must think clearly and logically; his main task is to solve problems, especially problems related to power and how to accumulate it. Being tuned in and sensitive is not essential to a man because it will be difficult to think logically if you let people's feelings interfere. Success—being a competitive worker—will be difficult if you become too aware of others' emotions, so it is important that you put rationality above feelings. Leave emotionality and sensitivity to women; they are better at it than you."

These instructions affect all children—less so now than in years past, but they are still a pervasive influence on our young. Even if the household in which we were raised did not particularly subscribe to this point of view, there still are school, television, the movies, the newspapers, and other adults and children to reinforce these points of view.

Of course, every person has had different role training and influences operating in his life. The point is that no man is free of them. How does this early-life, basic training affect men's eventual character? Naturally, the effect varies, but let me draw you three caricatures of the outcome of these childhood instructions when driven to three different extremes: "The Sex Machine," "The Workaholic," and "Cool, Calm, and Collected."

Men Are Sex Machines

One of women's major complaints about men concerns their intense interest in sex. Each of the following comments comes from a different distraught woman.

"His only emotional outlet is sexual. I only know he is feeling something when he is passionately interested in getting into my pants."

"Unless sex is in the picture, he is not interested; if a woman is not sexually attractive, she doesn't count. With him sex is first, everything else follows."

"He only touches me when he is interested in having sex; if I touch him, he assumes it is sexual—a come-on. I am deathly afraid of showing any affection for him because I cannot get him to be affectionate back without it becoming a sexual thing."

"It seems that as long as he is turned on to me, he has energy for me. The moment that he comes, he goes away; he either falls asleep, starts reading, or rolls over. I feel utterly erased as if I didn't exist."

These descriptions may be extreme, but most men are

aware of the kind of sexual focus we often operate under. For some reason we are compelled to pursue women for the purpose of having intercourse with them. We may mask this obsession and try to be civilized, or we may be blatant about it. We may be successful at it, or we may be utter failures; nevertheless, we seem to have that tendency to think of women as sexual opportunities and often little else. And they know it.

Varying reasons have been given for this tendency. Some say that it is a specifically male urge having to do with inborn aggression and the biological drive to procreate. Another theory is that since men are trained to suppress feelings, the only feelings that remain are the powerful genital sensations that the sexual act provides. When a man meets a woman who doesn't enjoy his advances, the combination of his tendency to be unaware of people's feelings and his drive to have intercourse results in a disregard for the annoyance he causes her. This relentless pursuit of sexual encounter is the source of women's complaints that they appear to be mere objects for his sexual needs; hence, women's accusation that men perceive them as "sexual objects."

Another more charitable explanation for men's constant sexual search is that men have an insatiable curiosity to experience women's intimate, emotional, sexual response. The reason given for this is that men are cut off, alienated from their own emotions by their upbringing. Women's feelings, therefore, become enormously attractive and endlessly fascinating. Being in the presence of women's loving energy is overwhelmingly pleasurable. To be able to generate such feelings in women is simply wonderful, and to be able to feel them intimately is sublime. But when a man pursues a woman just for the sake of this experience, he probably doesn't care particularly who she is, and in the process she will justifiably feel used.

Women are not entirely innocent in the process of their objectification. Many women are so concerned with their looks and their attractiveness to men that they turn *themselves* into objects. They put so much emphasis on clothes, makeup, and charming and attractive behavior, that in the end no real person can be discerned. A man trying to relate to this kind of a woman will be relating to a front; he can hardly be blamed if he has problems thinking of her as a person. He may desire her, but he won't be able to understand her. He may be able to have sex with her, but he won't know how to make love to her.

It is hard for men to imagine what the experience of sexual objectification is like for a woman. We assume that if we were on the receiving end of that kind of attention we would be pleased and flattered. It's difficult for us to understand why some women find it so hurtful and insulting, especially since they don't all and don't *always* seem to feel that way. The only comparable experience for men is the way we are objectified as breadwinners and meal tickets. As we evaluate women by the size of their breasts, we are likely to be evaluated by the size of our wallets. We too are flattered when we are admired for our earning capacities, but in the end it is a demeaning appraisal foisted on us by the same sex roles that turn us into sex machines. And that is not all.

The objectification of men's bodies by women is progressing rapidly. Lately, role reversals in the movies and other media are showing women lusting after long legs, flat tummies, and powerful "lats" on men's semi-naked, young bodies. Men are being handed a dose of their

13

own medicine. This is, I believe, all to the good. It's probably the single most effective way of instilling some understanding in us of how it feels to be treated like a hunk of meat. Perhaps as women turn a jaundiced eye on our imperfect bodies, we will develop more tolerance and understanding for the female condition.

Men Are Workaholics

Another major complaint about men is that they care about their work above all else. The following complaints come from a number of different women.

"When I talk about how I feel, his eyes glaze over. He may appear to be listening, but he is gone to a faraway land of business charts and stock options which I never hope to enter."

"He never has any fun; he's always thinking of his work."

"I come in a definite second in his life; first, the work, then, maybe if there is time, me."

"Work, eat, watch TV, sleep, that's all he seems to want to do. When we go on vacation, it takes him all the time to wind down. By the time the vacation is over, he is getting into it."

"He works two jobs, and when he comes home, he fixes things around the house. I guess I can't complain when he works so hard, but I hate it anyway. Why can't he relax and enjoy life?"

"Carl's interests are focused on work, success, himself. He doesn't care about me, just himself and his ego. He is a good husband, I suppose, but if husbanding requires interest in my feelings, forget it."

Mr. Workaholic is the extension, to grotesque extremes, of the childhood instructions to be a responsible caretaker, boosted by the encouragement men receive

14

when they fulfill that role. Men are taught that their tasks in life are to provide for a wife and family and to be as secure, rich, and powerful as possible. Consequently, men are astonished when women question these priorities. After all, women expect men to work and take care of them. If a man were to consider putting aside his responsibilities, he would likely be overwhelmed with guilt, which itself might drive him back to his work until he got sick or dropped dead.

Relaxing, having fun, letting go—it's just not that easy. Some drug, usually alcohol, may help to bring the workaholic down enough to make relaxation possible. Unfortunately, the alcohol wears off, more is needed, and eventually he falls asleep or gets drunk. His workaholism may lead to alcoholism or some other form of drug addiction. Lately, such men have been using cocaine to increase their work output, though coffee and cigarettes still are the most traditional workmates. Joy is hard to come by. Fun and relaxation are not this man's common experience, though he longs for and pursues them in his sexual life and drug use.

Women are usually ambivalent about men's intense focus on their work. At first it seems desirable. But when the work takes the love and joy out of the relationship, hurt, anger, and resentment replace the initial acceptance.

Janet, a 40-year-old housewife, said this about her husband's obsession with work:

"Max is a stockbroker, and he brings his work home. I used to bring him tea and sit and read while he worked in the evenings. I never thought to complain. But as the years passed and there seemed to be no end to his work, I began to hate it. I suppose that I expected it to be less as he did better, but it actually got worse. I had no

15

husband and began to question the whole thing. As far as I am concerned, I don't care how well he does. It doesn't do me any good after a certain point if he is never there for me."

Women want men to balance home life and work in such a way that neither their security nor their relationship is threatened. When a man loves a woman, he probably would appreciate being able to establish such a balance; to do so usually requires ongoing discussion and the cooperation of both partners.

Men Are Emotionally Retarded

A third major complaint about men is that their emotional responses are hard to understand.

"With Don when things are okay, I usually feel that I know him. Then suddenly he does something that I just don't understand. If I try to find out why, I just hit a brick wall. He won't, or can't, tell me how he feels. His reasons don't make sense to me, and I keep thinking, 'If he only told me how he feels, I'd understand.'"

"Sometimes I can tell he is angry, but he denies it," said Sue, 35, married to Jack, a truck driver, 39. "Sometimes I am amazed at his lack of normal response. When I expect him to be scared, he is not. When I need nurturing, he gets turned off. Then he gets depressed and doesn't know why. I just give up trying to make sense of him."

"He tries to appear cool, but all he is is hard to read, and hard to deal with. I know something is happening, and I can even guess what it is, but he denies my guesses, and claims not to be feeling anything. So I am left in the dark. After a while I get angry. The angrier I get the cooler he gets. It makes me feel like a helpless child. I want to hit him so he'll feel something. Then he looks

16

hurt and scared. But would he admit to it? Not on your life." So speaks Anne, 29, about her lover of four years.

"He never says, 'I love you!' I know he does, or at least I think he does, and he does try to hint that he does, but he never comes right out and lets me off the hook by looking me in the eye and saying straight out and without hesitation, 'I love you.'"

The image of the totally unruffled man of action, the silent type, tall, dark, and handsome, in control of his feelings, of women, of any situation—the man who never loses his cool, certainly never cries (unless someone dies and then maybe), and only gets angry when totally self-righteous—is a powerful stereotype that we are constantly exposed to on movie and TV screens, in novels, magazines, and comic books. This image, when adopted by a real person, produces a human being who is easiest to relate to at a distance; the closer one gets, the harder he is to like. Because he is human, he really does have feelings. But he doesn't acknowledge them even to himself. Instead, he denies with singularity of purpose that he needs, hurts, hates, loves, fears, and hopes. He resists any and all attempts to bring him to deal with his feelings.

The reason for this is simply that he has been told in a multitude of ways, since early childhood, that feelings are a weakness that men should not indulge. He is trying to be a good man in the best way he knows how. When his feelings get the upper hand—often in the form of anger or in bouts of great depression and guilt—he regards this as a breakdown of essential controls and quickly tries to bring matters back to normal. When he fails, he may have a nervous breakdown, and when he gets close to being in love, he withdraws.

Women who relate to these kinds of men often feel

sorry for them and tolerate their coldness and lack of feeling. But eventually, once again, tolerance turns into disappointment, hurt, and anger that will affect the relationship. Men who find themselves creating an emotional gap in their relationships would do well to concentrate on becoming more aware and expressive of their own and others' emotional lives. Later on in this book we will see how that can be done.

Such male characteristics as described above are seldom found in their pure state in the real world. More likely, parts of them are found in all of us. Every man has a little of the sex machine, the workaholic, and the cool dude in him in different proportions at different times of his life. I explore them here because they are the male stereotypes that women complain about and because none of the three is a particularly effective way to be if one wants satisfying, intimate relationships with women. Each one has its initial appeal. After all, a man who is irresistibly sexy, who works hard and successfully, and who is in control of this chaotic world we live in is an attractive prospect. The drawbacks of this approach to life don't come out until he hangs out for a while, and we see that he is obsessed with sex, success, and control, and that glamorous as he appeared in the twilight of romantic encounters, he is not quite as appealing in the sustained light of long-term intimacy.

Ask yourself these questions: Does any of the above seem to describe me? Do women's complaints ring a bell of recognition? Can you say that you are not affected by the patterns of manhood that I describe?

As a man you are probably influenced by one or more of these male roles, and you probably have suffered in your relationships with women (and men) because of them, as have I. This is only natural. But it is not necessary, and if we are so inclined, we can do something to change it.

Let us now turn to what women want and don't want, like and dislike in their sexual lives.

CHAPTER 3 | LEARNING

TO BE A

BETTER LOVER

When the subject of female sexuality overcame the taboos that prevented it from being discussed, let alone written about, the first wave of so-called expert information was ludicrously inaccurate. Women did not have orgasms, we were told, or they had them automatically when men did. Women lost their minds with lust and they became addicted to masturbation and clitoral stimulation, or they were content merely to satisfy their man, requiring no orgasm for themselves. Theories about women's sexuality ranged widely and in contradictory directions.

Lately, especially since women's sexuality became a concern of the women's liberation movement, the information has become more accurate and reliable.

What Women Like and Don't Like

The single most informative source on the subject of women's sexual preferences is *The Hite Report: A Nationwide Study of Female Sexuality*. This book could make

20

difficult reading for men, not only because it is long and at times complicated but also because it paints an unflattering portrait of the male lovemaking style. It is a shock to see how women view us as lovers.

When women were asked, "How have most men had sex with you?" they described their experiences with men as basically, "kiss, suck, fuck, snore." In a seemingly endless litany, scores of women recalled their typical experiences.

"Small amount of foreplay, then intercourse till he comes. The end." ". . . Speed demon." "Take what you can and don't give any." "Getting on and getting it over as soon as possible." "An excess of activity." "Slam, bang, thank you ma'am." "Insert A into B. Dull, dull, dull, dull."

To the question "Who decides when it's over?" the answers were: "Dick Power, the penis decides." "He does, as he ejaculates." "He goes to sleep at once and snores."

I was personally pained when reading these complaints because I had to recognize situations where these descriptions could fit my own behavior. Hopefully, it wasn't ever as crude as "Insert A into B," but I didn't like seeing myself described, even remotely, by Hite's disgruntled subjects. In any case, I recommend reading this book as a sobering introduction to the basic facts about what is wrong sexually between men and women.

The following are summaries of the findings especially important for men to be aware of:

—Only 30 percent of women had orgasms during intercourse.

—Only 11 percent of the women who didn't have an orgasm during intercourse said that they felt okay about it. The rest felt anywhere from annoyed to very upset. And 70 percent of them held the man responsible.

—82 percent of women masturbated, and of these 92 percent achieved orgasm.

—Overwhelmingly, women wanted sex with feeling.

That means that the majority of women whom you, dear reader, have had, or will have intercourse with:

1. Will not have an orgasm.

2. Will feel bad about it.

3. Would be able to achieve orgasm through some form of additional stimulation.

4. Will blame you for their failure to achieve orgasm.

5. Will forgive almost anything if you show a capacity for communication at the emotional level.

Hite's findings confirm with the weight of statistical evidence what has been suspected by many about the relationship between the sexes and about what women want—namely, to repeat: *Women want good sex with feeling*.

Feeling here means not just any feelings, but first and foremost, feelings of love, affection, tenderness—feelings that feel good.

It is fairly clear by now what women consider lousy lovemaking—to wit: a man who after a minute's foreplay, finds his way into her, thrusts vigorously for sixty seconds, comes, and is fast asleep and snoring by the end of the third minute, leaving her lying on the wet spot. You might call him a three-minute man.

While such men are on their way to becoming extinct, you get the idea of what they are like. You can be sure that our three-minute man's sex life isn't very active, since there are few women in this day and age who would be willing to lie still for such lovemaking (especially more than once).

Why Women Don't Want to Have Sex (As Often As Men)

It has taken countless centuries for men to realize that women enjoy sex every bit as much as (if not more than) we do. For the longest time, it was commonly believed that normal women did not, could not, and would not find sex pleasurable. The wondrous facts of the female orgasm, long hidden from view, have finally become common knowledge: Women definitely want and most certainly do enjoy sex. Then why is it that as a rule they don't want to *do* it as much as we do? The reasons are many, though any one woman may have her own assortment. Let me list them in the order of frequency with which they've been mentioned to me.

WOMEN TAKE SEX MORE PERSONALLY THAN MEN.

To men, sex is often a short-lived event that doesn't necessarily involve the heart as much as it does for women. Consequently, men can have sex more casually—with someone they hardly know or don't even like, during or after an argument, or in spite of other unresolved emotional issues. To men, sexuality is simply more limited to just that—sexuality—than it often is for women. Thus, women are more hesitant to have sex for fear of the deeper emotional consequences potentially associated with sexual relations—hurt, heartbreak, or self-reproach.

"My problem," said one woman, "is that if I really let myself go with a man, I'm liable to fall in love with him. He may be a jerk, and to him what happened was about as important as a warm handshake, but I haven't been able to help myself stay detached. It's not worth it, believe me, no matter how good."

It's hard for a man to put himself in a woman's shoes

23

and imagine how different she may feel about having sex than he. If she has no moral reservations, why doesn't she just go ahead? We tend to interpret her reluctance as some form of tease or power play, a way of dominating us or using our needs to her advantage. But sex is not experienced in the same way by men and women. Quite obviously, sex happens inside a woman while it happens outside a man; it is a more intimate, vulnerable, private matter for a woman, and we need to be sympathetic to that fact.

"Ever since we first met," said Mary about her husband Chuck, "he has been ready to have sex before I was. He wanted to have sex on our first date. I liked him as much as he liked me, it was love at first sight, but I just wasn't ready to open up that fast. Later on, when we know we are going to get it on, he wants to get to it in ten minutes when I want an hour. If we just had a fight, especially, I want to make up before we make love; to him, making love *is* making up. I just have the feeling that it doesn't mean the same to him as it means to me."

MEN ARE OFTEN NOT VERY GOOD LOVERS.

Frequently, a woman may have had the experience of unsatisfying sex with a man while he seemed quite content. Perhaps she hasn't come, perhaps she has been squashed by an enthusiastic man who assumed and kept the proverbial missionary, man-above position. Perhaps she has experienced that men's egos are highly sensitive and that they react badly, even angrily, to suggestions for improvement. Possibly she has noticed that men are disgusted by her genitals, their odor, her menses. He may have fallen asleep shortly after he came, leaving her feeling lonely and frustrated; men may have

24

been cold and lacked sensitivity, or they may have been violent when thwarted. She may have been raped.

In short, she may not have enjoyed previous sexual encounters, has no reason to expect better, and doesn't want to have to deal with inept lovemaking, especially with a man whose interest may be purely recreational.

She may feel, as one woman put it, "I hardly know the guy. If I could have been sure that sex would be good, I would have gone for it, but let's face it, chances are it wouldn't and he wouldn't even realize it. So then I have to get rid of him. His feelings will be hurt, so I'll have to spend time being considerate and sensitive if he sulks, or I'll have to fight him off if he can't take no for an answer. I can't bear to think of the hassle."

PAINFUL SEX, IRRITATIONS, INFECTIONS, V.D.

Lately, there has been an epidemic increase of genital herpes. This disease is far more painful for women than for men and can also endanger the health of children during birth. Women have reason to fear other genital infections as well. In addition to herpes, there are yeast infections, trichomonas, and chlamidia, all of which men carry from woman to woman and which affect them hardly at all. Gonorrhea and syphilis are more likely to go undetected in women and gonorrhea is more difficult to treat in women than in men. Finally, there is AIDS (acquired immune deficiency syndrome). Even though AIDS threatens primarily gay men, it is beginning to affect heterosexual men and women, and men are presently overwhelmingly the carriers. Consequently, women have more reason to avoid casual sex than do men.

"It took me years to realize what was happening, but it turns out that every time I make love to somebody

25

new, I wind up with some kind of crotch itch. Only after I have been making love to a guy for a while, it seems that I don't react this way. It must be that my vaginal environment has to get used to him. I don't know, but that does not help when it comes to getting it on casually." So spoke a woman who had regretfully decided that though she enjoyed casual sex, she had to give it up.

So again, we need to put ourselves in the woman's place and understand why she may be hesitant when we are hot, how—though she may like us and may want to have sex as much as we do—she chooses to abstain.

FEAR OF PREGNANCY

While the above reasons apply mainly to casual sex, fear of pregnancy is a constant dampener of women's sexual activity, whether casual or not. The fact remains that the consequences of pregnancy as well as much of the responsibility for birth control fall upon the woman. While it may seem to men that modern birth control methods make pregnancy a problem of the past, such is actually not the case. The pill and the intra-uterine device (IUD), two of the most reliable and unobtrusive methods, have uncomfortable and potentially serious side effects. Cancer from the pill and pelvic infections from the IUD are potentially life-threatening repercussions for women. Many women are justifiably unwilling to submit themselves to those risks.

"For a while, in the sixties, I thought the problem was solved," said a woman in her late thirties. "I took the pill, and although it had definite side effects, I thought, what the heck, it's worth it. But then all that research started to come out, and even though they tell you now that it's only a problem if you smoke, I just don't trust

26

them. I'm afraid of them and I'm not willing to take a chance. It's too early to know for sure, and I don't trust doctors either. It doesn't seem that they care. As far as the IUD is concerned, forget it. A friend of mine had a baby on an IUD and another almost died of a pelvic infection. So I'm back to square one; birth control is a real problem and turns me off to sex."

This leaves women having to rely on methods that are less than perfect. Consequently, pregnancy is always a possibility no matter how remote. In the case of unwanted pregnancy, abortion is still an option. However, women realize that though they may be thankful for the right to terminate an unwanted pregnancy, an abortion is seldom anything but a painful, harrowing, and heartbreaking event. Abortion is completely outside of men's experience. Men's lack of understanding of the realities of birth control and abortion leads them to discount women's utterly understandable fear of careless intercourse and makes them intolerant of women's sexual reluctance.

A MATTER OF MORALS

Some women believe that sexual expression, whether casual or not, is wrong outside of marriage or even within it, unless it is designed to bring about children. For a woman who has these beliefs, sexuality is associated with a great deal more guilt than for men with similar beliefs. Men have always been indulged in their sins more than women have. Women who break sexual codes are called sluts; men are more than likely forgiven with a knowing smile, and are even admired.

LACK OF CONTROL

Least often mentioned but very important, in my opinion, is what the "normal" sexual experience between a man and a woman is supposed to be like. The assumption is that the man will be active and the woman passive.

Consequently, both partners enter into a sexual experience with the expectation that the man will call the shots and the woman will respond with pleasure. If he happens to make the right moves—that is, the moves that fit into her needs—events will progress satisfactorily. But if he goes too fast or too slow, too gently or too roughly, she usually doesn't have the knowledge, experience, or cultural permission to rectify matters or take the initiative to gain some control over the course of events. If she does assume more power in the situation, she incurs the real risk of being seen as sexually grasping and scaring the man into impotence, a recent phenomenon familiar to newly assertive women. If she doesn't assume power, she is likely to feel increasingly powerless and uncomfortable with the situation.

Her position is similar to that of a passenger in a car on a fast ride, another experience more familiar to women than men. When driving fast, the person in control is definitely going to have more fun. If the passenger doesn't happen to enjoy the ride at all, there are only two things she can do—relax and trust, or say something and risk getting into an argument with the driver— but either solution is not as good as getting into the driver's seat. Any man who wants to get a feel for what I'm talking about can start by offering the keys of his beloved car to an aggressive female driver and experiencing the difference between being in control and giving up control.

Fortunately, sex is different from driving, and control does not need to be exclusively in the hands of one or the other participant. In fact, the best sex probably occurs when control goes back and forth between partners, giving both of them the opportunity to experience the two sides of the control equation.

A woman may try to be a good sexual partner, but the dominance-submission relationship may not work for her and nothing she does within that equation may set it straight. Neither she nor her partner may realize that the reason for their difficulty is based on an assumption about who is in control, who leads and who follows, and who gets to set the beat of their sexual rhythm.

Who is in control is probably the single most important factor in whether the woman will have an orgasm. She may need oral sex, masturbation, or the woman-above position to climax. If she can have sex the way she likes it, she will probably be satisfied. The man, however, may get turned off by her aggressivity or not get what *he* needs—a rare but useful opportunity to experience what is a common event for women.

Sexual difficulties are usually blamed on the woman. It's very much like when she isn't able to follow the man's lead on the dance floor. Good sex, like good dancing, is said to depend on the woman being a good follower. As women become more powerful and less willing to follow, sexual disharmony may actually increase until men learn to follow and women learn to lead, all of which may take considerable time and effort.

29

Sexuality is a very delicate process easily spoiled by pain and anxiety. Repeated bouts with all of the minor and major hassles of sex can cause women to develop an automatic anxious response, which can put a damper on her desire and interfere with her pleasure. This process accounts for most so-called "female frigidity." Due to the caprice of anatomy, a woman who is not enjoying sex, unlike a man, can still have intercourse. Every time a person has bad, unpleasant sex, negative conditioning will accumulate, so women are more likely to lose their enjoyment of sex than men.

For all these reasons, most of the time that a woman and man meet, even if they are mutually attracted, the woman is likely to be less motivated to have sex. So, while a man tends to seek intercourse, a woman will tend to be more cautious, unless she's young and restless and inexperienced about the hassles of sexuality. When she has grown accustomed to a man's body, trusts him, and precautions to prevent conception have been taken, then orgasm becomes a likely and pregnancy an unlikely outcome of their lovemaking, and she may become less reluctant. But according to a survey of her readers, Ann Landers recently found that 75 percent of the women would gladly give up sex altogether and settle for nonsexual attention.

Some men and women who have read these lines have argued with the premise that men are more interested in sex than women. Their experiences seem to contradict that point of view. Married women, especially, complain that their husbands lose interest in sex. Some, usually very attractive young men, find that women are more interested in sex than they are. Women don't always have a tendency to shy away from sex.

Women complain of men's sexual passivity or coldness or of their tendency to become clinging and dependent. Men, too, have moral scruples, fears of becoming emotionally involved, and fears of becoming infected or impotent or being inept. There *are* women who complain about men's reluctance to have sex with them. But according to *The Hite Report on Male Sexuality*, they are in the minority. In Hite's own succinct words, "Men's major dissatisfaction—women don't want sex enough." She explains, "Only 11 percent of the 7,000 men who replied stated that they were fully satisfied with the frequency of sex."

What Can a Man Do?

When a man finds that he wants sex with a woman who doesn't, he needs to be sympathetic to her hesitation. He should accept the reasons for her reluctance and take them seriously. Instead of discounting her fears of pregnancy or disease, he should find out more and be sympathetic. He ought not to force himself on her, or try to talk her into having sex anyway. He needs to be aware of his own disappointment and hurt, but he should not withdraw his interest or resign himself or sulk. He can state his desire, but ought to allow her the freedom to choose without feeling pressured.

This is not easy for men to do, but it is what women want. Women don't like to be seduced or pressured, contrary to popular opinion. They may occasionally allow it, but a man who is willing to consider the reasons that deter a woman from sexual intercourse will find that his irresistible desire can become resistible and that his interest and loving concern for her can temper his wants. He will become less sexually needy, more loving.

31

She will have the room to assess her own sexual desire and assuage her fears and perhaps find that after all, she too wants to make sexual love.

In fact an interesting paradox develops. If a man is aggressively seductive and pushes his desire for sex, his chances of "scoring" may increase. Women can occasionally be intimidated into having sex, regardless of how much they may hate to be coerced in that manner. On occasion it may even happen, to a woman's surprise, that such a seduction develops into a good sexual experience.

On the other hand, a man who scrupulously avoids trying to pressure women may find that women will approach *him* instead. Women appreciate not being pressured for sex. Being relieved of such pressure often puts them in touch with their own desires so that, in the end, this approach may lead to a sexual relationship as often as a more aggressive one.

But while the frequency of sexual relations in the above two options may be the same, the quality will be vastly different. For one thing, the women a man relates to sexually will be different: If he is aggressive, the women will be passively going along; if he is laid back, they will actively desire him.

If he is pushy, the sexual relationships are likely to be short-lived and tense since the woman will eventually find a way of avoiding his unwanted advances. If he is not pushy, sexuality is more likely to continue and improve since she entered into it of her own accord. It will be more truly passionate and joyous, perhaps even earthshaking. Both will be more likely to climax fully and with abandon. They will have a better chance to experience intimacy. Regardless of whether they become long-term lovers, or friends, or turn out to be just

32

ships passing in the night, the experience of intimacy between them will bond their hearts, bringing a smile to their faces whenever recalled, forever a source of sweet energy and pleasure rather than shame and regret. Such mutually agreed-upon experiences can do a great deal to improve the overall climate in the relationships between men and women.

We know now that women want to be surrounded by romance, they like doing things together, intimate talk, holding hands, taking walks, being listened to. They want to make love, have orgasms, and spend time being close after making love. They like to be kissed on the mouth, vagina, all over; they like to be caressed, cuddled, cradled, and hugged.

More specifically, however, what a woman likes varies from woman to woman. Kissing, for instance, is preferred all the way from gentle to rough, from dry to wet, from long to short. Every woman has special parts of the body that she likes to have caressed in a specific way—except that at times she may want that particular part touched differently or not at all. In other words, if she usually likes soft caresses on her breast, she may at other times prefer them to be squeezed or maybe left completely alone. Or if at most times she does not like direct stimulation of her clitoris, she may desire it during intercourse.

Similarly, some women like intercourse but do not reach an orgasm from it, while others reach orgasms from intercourse but don't like it as much as cunnilingus or some other form of lovemaking. The same women who like intercourse while mildly aroused may not like it later when about to climax, or vice versa. It is not possible to give anything but a shopping list of women's preferences without falling into the error of gener-

33

alization. What any one woman will like will vary, depending partly on her mood, where she is, the phases of the moon, whom she is with and why.

Knowing that most women (more than 50 percent) do not achieve an orgasm through intercourse, and that a preferred method of climaxing is cunnilingus, doesn't necessarily tell a man what the woman he's with really wants. True, he won't climb on her and come in fifty seconds flat; that much both have learned to avoid. But he may still leave her high and dry because his information is incomplete. There is no handbook to turn to. The answer depends completely on soliciting information from her, being tuned in and attentive, and developing a sense for the rhythm and flow of the sexual dance. Let us turn now to some important steps in that dance.

CHAPTER 4

THE THREE

C'S OF

CUNNILINGUS

Cunnilingus is the foremost alternative to intercourse, mentioned repeatedly by women as a source of orgasmic satisfaction. In my opinion, it's a skill that any man who proposes to be a good lover needs to master. Because it is independent of the other major male sexual skill (maintaining an erection), it can be learned separately by any man—even one who may be troubled with impotence. Once learned, the awareness and sensitivity involved in helping a woman come to orgasm through cunnilingus will be beneficial during intercourse as well.

Cunnilingus puts two of the sexiest human organs, the clitoris and the head, in the closest possible contact—with the tongue, a highly sensitive, subtle, and powerful muscle, as the bridge between them. Perhaps it is the proximity of the brain to the tongue that makes cunnilingus an ideal situation in which to learn about women's sexual response. The tongue is precise in its movements, and the woman's reaction to it quickly re-

veals the effectiveness of its action; feedback is immediate.

While the tongue and lips are the protagonists in cunnilingus, the hands play important supporting roles.
Placed around her hips or on her belly or with one, two,
or three fingers in her vagina, the hands gather information about breath and muscular contractions as well
as adding to the stimulation. Finally, the ears pick up
breathing patterns and expressions of pleasure.

The three requirements of pleasurable and effective
cunnilingus are: being clean, comfortable, and communicative. If you wish to pursue cunnilingus to the
woman's orgasm, it's important to arrange for the three
C's of C.

CLEAN

Some men enjoy giving head to a woman whose genitals
are in a state of seasoned ripeness. That kind of appetite
will not go unnoticed and is likely to be appreciated.

Any man who doesn't have the taste for that kind of
passion should feel free to ask her to wash. The French,
who are knowledgeable about these matters, have bi-
dets for that purpose. In the absence of a bidet, a shower
or a bath or a warm washcloth are appropriate preludes
to oral sex. This is also an opportunity for a man to
wash his own genitals, something which is highly rec-
ommended to avoid spreading lesser vaginal infections.
In any case, cleanliness is a reasonable expectation, and
a man should not feel embarrassment or hesitation when
asking for it.

COMFORTABLE

It is essential for both partners to be comfortable, since
it can take a relatively long time for the woman to climax.

36

It is possible, in that time, to get a stiff neck or a cramp if one starts in an uncomfortable position. Giving head with one's neck bent as is required when the woman is lying on her back and the man is lying on his stomach can be very uncomfortable for some men. Both can lie on their sides, but this may be uncomfortable for the woman. Placing a pillow under her back may help. Another good position for comfort is with her hips at the edge of the bed and the man on the floor kneeling or even sitting up. This may be uncomfortable for a woman who needs to heave her legs up to come. If so, she can wrap her legs around him, put her feet on his shoulders, or scoot back on the bed enough to put her feet up. At any rate, make sure you are both comfortable and you'll be able to take your time, which is essential.

COMMUNICATIVE

This is the age of communication. Right? Yet, for some reason people feel acute embarrassment about discussing their precise wants and dislikes during lovemaking.

"Many is the time," one woman confessed about her lovemaking with her husband, "when I have made love painfully and was not able to say anything about it. He was sucking too hard, but he seemed to enjoy it so much that I did not want to interrupt. I was able to come all right, but I know that I could have asked him to go easy and really enjoyed it more."

So ask: "Is this too hard? Too fast? Are you comfortable?" If the answer is "Sure," it might help to make really sure. "Good, I want to make sure because I want you to really enjoy this. Let me know if you get uncomfortable in any way, okay?" Whenever you wonder about how she is feeling or whether she is enjoying what you are doing or whether there is something you can do to

37

improve it, ask and ask again until asking becomes second nature. Paradoxically, being able to ask will result in your having to ask less and less as you become more sensitive to the clues of her pleasures.

The Art of Cunnilingus

Let us now get to the nuts and bolts of the matter, speak the unspeakable, and talk about just how it is done.

Find the opening of the vagina and then run your tongue around it. Taste your lover's wetness and learn to appreciate its flavor. Do this slowly, listening to and feeling her responses. Put your hands on her hips or breasts and hold them or caress them. Don't expect anything in particular, just pay attention. Let your mind drift, play a tune or a rhythm with your tongue and lips, relax and enjoy her reactions.

Eventually, in good time, move your tongue upwards until you feel her clitoris. The clitoris may be heavily hooded and small or exposed and large or somewhere in between, so you may not be sure whether you have found it. It may be helpful here to realize that the clitoris is somewhat like a tiny uncircumcised penis, a shaft with a tip that is very sensitive on the underside. The shaft is covered by a retractable layer of skin, which may cover it completely or leave the tip exposed.

If you think you have found the clitoris but aren't sure, ask, "Is that your clitoris?" She may say yes or she may show you with her fingers where it really is. Ask her to tell you when you are getting warm and when you are right on it.

The clitoris may or may not be erect; you won't necessarily be able to tell when you first find it because a small erect clitoris is not that different from a large one

38

that is not erect. However, that's not important. Like a man, a woman can have a clitoral erection and not be turned on or be quite turned on and not be fully erect.

With the tip of your tongue look for that sensitive area under the tip of the clitoris. With one or two fingers, you can pull up the hood while you are doing this, which will help you to get under it. When you find the clitoris and its tip, be careful to be very gentle because for some women direct stimulation of the tip of the clitoris can feel too strong, even painful. Be aware of her reaction. Explore the tip, the shaft, the vaginal labia and opening, while listening to her response, or suck on the whole clitoris. Eventually stop and ask her how she feels. "Is it too strong? Can it be stronger? Is it right? Can you tell me what I can do?" If it is not right, try again. Ask again and try again. That will give you an idea of how strong a stimulation she likes.

You now have the basic requirements for giving good head: she is clean and sweet smelling, you are comfortable, and you are communicating with each other. You have found the clitoris. Now you are ready to begin in earnest, and from now on there are no rules except to tune in and go with the flow.

1. It's important not to think too much about her orgasm. It's much better to just have fun, not intense pleasure, but fun, like chasing a kitten or flying a kite, driving a curvy road or dancing the samba. In the process you'll both get high on sexual energy.

To enjoy dancing or playing with a kitten you need a responsive, lively partner. The same is true here. The more your lover can openly express how she is reacting to your stimulation, the more you feel her move or be still, the more you hear her moan or squeal, the more you will be able to join her in the dance, get lost in the whirlwind, and get high chasing her pleasure with your tongue.

If for some reason she is not giving you any feedback—not making noise or moving—or if her reaction becomes monotonous, you should probably stop. Explain you aren't sure she is enjoying it and ask that she let you know what she likes and what she doesn't like.

2. Don't continue beyond the point that you are enjoying it yourself. If you are getting a stiff neck or a sore tongue or if you are beginning to get bored, don't go on. Do something else for a while. Intercourse may keep her excitement high, or you can use your fingers while kissing her breasts, or use a vibrator. Tell her what you want to do and find out if it's okay with her. Or ask her what she wants to do. After a while you can return to cunnilingus. Or you may decide not to.

3. In the midst of your tongue play, your lover may go from a state of sexual arousal to a new, pre-orgasmic stage. The most noticeable change will be an increase in muscular tension around her pelvis alternating with short periods of relaxation followed by increasing tension. Her back may arch, or her legs stiffen; she may pull your hair or push herself against you. She may begin to tremble. She might increase her sounds of pleasure or she may become very still. This means that she is within reach of an orgasm. At this point you must follow her lead: she needs steady and accurate stimulation to accumulate the sexual tension that will bring her over the edge. Don't increase the tempo or intensity of your activity, just maintain it steadily and in close responsiveness to her movements. Think of yourself rolling a marble uphill with your tongue. Don't let it roll down; you need to stay with it to get over the top.

At this point, when orgasm becomes the objective, what your partner does is as important as what you do. You can only provide 50 percent of the stimulation; she needs to do the rest. There is no magic formula; you can only do your best, and the rest is up to her and to circumstances. The day, time, and place may be right or they may not be. If she comes easily (and some women come far more easily than others), there should be no problem. If not, what you do may or may not be sufficient. You'll find out through experience and trial and error.

Sometimes, she will lose the accumulated tension, perhaps due to the overly intense concentration on her genitals, which may make her self-conscious, perhaps because your stimulation became too intense or not intense enough, or because you lost the beat, or she started thinking about her orgasm and became anxious about how long it was taking. If so, continue as long as you are still up to it, and if you aren't, stop, do something else, explain that you need a change. Suggest that she use a vibrator or her hand to bring herself to orgasm. If she does, you can take over when she gets close to it, or you can just watch her come. Kiss her all over, play with her breasts and enjoy her pleasure. While all of this is going on, learn as much as you can about what her orgasm is like—what are her pre-orgasmic movements and sounds, how does she build up the tension to climax, and when she reaches the top, how does she ride the crest, and how does she take the down side of the roller coaster. Not only will all of this be a pleasure to observe, but it will give you valuable information for the next time, because every person has a characteristic way of coming that tends to repeat itself. Familiarity with her pattern will be helpful on future occasions.

So, your work is cut out for you. Women have made it clear that they want their men to be willing and able to give them head. Now it's up to you to go down to the occasion with the knowledge that it will make her happy and that it will make you all the more desirable to her.

CHAPTER 5

HOW TO

KEEP AN

ERECTION

A very common response to the question "What do you want from a man, sexually?" was that he be able to maintain an erection long enough for the woman to have an orgasm.

For men there are two major problems regarding erections. First, is getting the erection. Second, keeping it. Frequently, a man can get an erection but cannot maintain it because of a tendency to come soon after being inside a woman.

Getting It Up

If you are a man who has a problem getting an erection, the first thing to remember is that if you ever do become aroused enough to get hard, then your equipment is in working condition. The reason why you are not getting hard with a woman on any particular occasion is psychological or, as the shrinks say, in your head (the one on your shoulders). Unless you have a hormonal dis-

43

ease, diabetes, some sort of brain lesion, low blood pressure, or are abusing alcohol or other drugs—all of which can be physical reasons for impotence—your incapacity to get an erection is psychological.

So, if you have ever had an erection—whether in sexual situations, or in the middle of the night, or in the morning when you wake up—you are not physically impotent.

There are two main psychological reasons why a man can't get an erection when he wants it.

1. He is not turned on to the woman. This is actually a healthy response. Men are accustomed to believing that if a woman is willing, a man should be able, regardless of how he feels about her. But it is quite possible that a man will find himself in bed with a woman to whom he is not really attracted. He may have gotten involved with her out of the male tendency to collect women as a way to stroke his ego, or he may be going along with her desire to have sex out of an unwillingness to do a very un-male thing and turn her down. So here he is with a woman he may or may not like, but is not really sexually turned on to. Not surprisingly he can't get hard.

In the past, perhaps in younger years, he may have been able to get a hard-on with anybody, any time, any place; a condition that is, after all, a sign of sexual immaturity. So he's growing up.

"When I had the experience of a man not getting an erection, my first reaction was that he wasn't turned on to me. First I took it personally, but he was very nice about it. He didn't get all upset but just kissed and cuddled me, and we slept the night together. Eventually, we did make love, but it was more a friendly fuck

44

than real hot. We got to be real good friends. Sex was never that important, and eventually we both found more passionate loves. When you think of it, when a man can't get hard it's no different than a woman not getting wet, and that happens a lot, doesn't it?"

A man's lack of arousal would, in fact, be far better tolerated if he were a woman. We are sympathetic when a woman can't respond to a man she is not attracted to, but we don't grant ourselves that privilege. We are, after all, men, and we have our responsibilities—one of which (we imagine) is to satisfy the women who need us.

Frequently, a man may not be sufficiently aroused, and thus he may have a problem getting an erection on the first two or three nights with a woman. This is certainly understandable—as understandable as a woman not having an orgasm on the first few sexual encounters with a man. We need only acknowledge the fact without embarrassment, and make love in other ways.

2. He is anxious about getting an erection. Fear and sexual arousal are physiologically incompatible. Maybe Mother Nature figured that it would be inconvenient for a man with an erection to run from an attacking tiger. In any case, they don't tend to happen together.

"The first time in my life that I couldn't get it up was at a sex party. I didn't know anybody at the party, and this woman who had just made love to this guy called me over and wanted me to fuck her. I had been attracted to her all evening, so it didn't even occur to me that I might have a problem. To my surprise I didn't get instantly hard; in fact, the harder I tried the softer I got. Eventually, I had an ejaculation with no erection, which

45

was totally new to me. The interesting thing is that ever since that time I get worried about getting it up in other situations."

If a man is anxious about his erection, his anxiety will become a factor in preventing him from getting one. If he fails to get an erection, his anxiety increases and so can his impotence. If this is combined with a partner who is unsympathetic or unattractive to him, a vicious cycle can develop until impotence becomes absolute.

Consequently, the solution for impotence is to have sex with women who are both attractive to you and sympathetic to your plight. Tell them of your anxiety. Women are familiar with the problem of being unable to have an orgasm. They are more likely to appreciate you if you are open and make yourself vulnerable about the situation than if you are secretive and defensive.

This kind of understanding and support is, in fact, the function of a professional sex therapist or surrogate. Such professionals can provide a sympathetic sexual opportunity. If your morals and your pocketbook will permit and if you live where such help is available, it's worth trying if you have a problem with erections.

Often, a man's erection is incomplete rather than absent. The penis may not be completely hard, but nevertheless it is hard enough to insert in the vagina. Men tend to feel that such a "half mast" isn't worthy of a woman's attention, but they are mistaken. It's really okay to rub a semihard penis against a woman's vagina and even to stuff it into her. Doing this will probably arouse both of you enough for nature to follow her course. Remember that lesbians are able to have totally satisfying sex without aid of a penis at all. They do quite well, thank you, and one of the ways they bring each

46

other to orgasm is to rub their pubic bones against each other, thereby stimulating their clitorises.

In any case, on the subject of soft penises, one woman said, "I like coming with a soft penis. It feels nurturing, and there are times when I don't like being banged. You get to feel more, actually. I like to feel the erection happening inside me."

The point here is that dealing with "impotence" through easygoing openness, communication, and creativity will practically guarantee that the problem will eventually go away. It's anxiety, secretiveness, and mental rigidity that are responsible for so-called "impotence."

One commonly asked question is worth answering here: "Why is it that sometimes I find myself with a woman whom I consider perfect in every way, and I can't get it up?"

This hellish situation has been known to happen on occasion. There are, as we have seen, several possible reasons. One is anxiety. The excited lover may, at the threshold of his cherished fantasy come true, suddenly begin to question his own worth and capacity. With this paragon of beauty lying receptively before him, he may have a sudden pang of doubt, which strikes terror into his heart and penis. If so, he needs to relax; extremely beautiful women are not unaccustomed to this phenomenon. Let him think about how much he likes her as a person and forget how beautiful she is. Let him kiss her face and breasts, caress her tenderly, speak to her with affection. Anxiety will melt away and lovemaking will happen in the end.

But perhaps the problem is different. Maybe, as beautiful as she is, this woman isn't all that sexy. Maybe she is not turned on either. I know this can be a blow to the ego. "I stood before paradise and was not man enough to tread upon it," you are likely to tell yourself. Well, let the fact that she was at least willing be a salve to your wounds and remember that a sense of humor can go a long way toward resolving the problem one way or another.

I know of a man who solved the problem by talking to his cock as a peasant would to his reluctant donkey, complaining at the same time to the expectant woman of its insensate stubbornness. I won't tell you what the donkey's precise response was, but I can tell you that in the end, it hardly mattered.

Keeping It There

Many men get an erection readily enough but have difficulty in preventing orgasm soon after penetration. The feeling of being inside a woman is so welcome, sensuous, and overwhelmingly delicious that we simply lose control and want to let go. Letting go is, after all, what sex is supposed to be about; one can hardly blame us for doing so when what we yearn for finally becomes reality.

Unfortunately, most women, even if they enjoy the man's ecstasies, are not able to be wholly empathetic to this abandon. They would like us to stay with them until they can climax too, so we must learn to accommodate them.

You may respond by suggesting that it is all right for the man to come first and then help the woman. While this is theoretically correct, it doesn't work very well in reality. The problem is, as women have noticed, the usual male response to orgasm is slumber. Because of

the expenditure of our precious bodily fluids or whatever, we often want to sleep soon after ejaculation. Also,
intercourse or other lovemaking can become boring or
even painful after orgasm, for both men and women.
So it's wise that when one climaxes, the other follow
close behind. Men generally come easier than women.
Consequently, it's simply a good idea for the woman
to climax first. And that requires that a man learn to
develop some staying power.

Learning is all it takes. To learn, you need practice.
What you need to practice is simply stopping stimulation in time to prevent orgasm. In other words, any
sexually healthy person will have an orgasm if sufficiently and properly stimulated. It is basically good that
you are so strongly excited when you are inside your
lover. It would be a shame to try to change that. When
men control their ejaculation by counting backward by
thirteens from five thousand, or by reviewing in their
minds the component parts of a motorcycle engine, they
are going about it the wrong way; the consequence may
be a "wooden penis" on an absent man, which most
women will not necessarily appreciate.

The solution is not to become rigid and controlling
but to come to the verge of orgasm and stop, pull back,
or, if necessary, out. Under extreme circumstances, it
can be effective to use the "squeeze" technique invented
by Masters and Johnson, which is simply to grip your
penis around its neck between the head and the shaft
until it loses the ejaculatory excitement. Personally, I
consider this approach somewhat brutal, even if effective, since lesser measures will work well enough without such violence.

Basically, I recommend that the man (preferably on

49

top where he has better control) slowly insert his penis and carefully approach the "point of no return." Just before that point comes, he should stop or pull out until his excitement subsides. Then he can start again, stop, start again, stop, and so on. If he fails to control his orgasm, he went too far. He needs to figure out that watershed point of no return, which may take several trials. The more often he does this, the more control he will gain over his ejaculation. Although this technique can be practiced while masturbating, what is most desirable here is a sympathetic partner who is willing to be patient, communicative, and creative.

Eventually, and this may take six months to a year of fairly constant practice, a man will be able to control his ejaculation during intercourse by varying the rhythm or amplitude of his thrusts while keeping up his lover's excitement. He will come to the edge of excitement and literally experience an orgasm without ejaculating, after which his arousal will subside somewhat. He can then thrust again and maintain this process indefinitely.

Very often a man's incapacity to prevent ejaculation is connected with infrequent sex. In such situations it's a good idea to plan to have two orgasms. The first orgasm can be through masturbation, fellatio, or intercourse. The second orgasm will be a lot easier to control than the first one.

Some women find it frustrating to stop and go, stop and go, in this fashion. The man must be aware of this and continue to stimulate her manually or orally while calming himself down. If he can prevent his orgasm without withdrawing by lying very still, the pressure of his pubic bone on her clitoris with some finger play may keep her aroused. She may even come. At this time, of course, he can happily let go, since all of this self-control is really designed to give her enough time to reach a climax.

This reinforces a very important point—maintaining an erection during intercourse involves the woman as much as the man. If the woman isn't enjoying herself and working her way toward an orgasm, the prolongation of intercourse becomes pointless. Aimless intercourse is all right for a while, but eventually a coordination between the two partners has to occur, or the man will be tempted to let go. He needs to know where she is, that she wants him to go on, and that what he is doing feels good. One way to do this is to agree mutually that he won't voluntarily come unless it is okay with her.

"Can I come?"
"Not yet, just a little longer . . ."
"Are you close?"
"Maybe. Let's keep going."
"Okay, but I've got to stop for a bit."
"Fine, I'm having great fun."

"Oh oh, can I come now?"
"Do you really want to?"
"It would be nice."
"Okay. Don't move and let me make you come."

"That was great."
"Yeah, guess what, I came too," or
"I loved it. Now it's my turn—eat me," or
"That's great, my turn next time, let's just cuddle."

51

A man who learns both these skills—cunnilingus and maintaining an erection—is likely to find that the women he relates to sexually will have orgasms easier and of-tener—while he will increase enjoyment of his own. But the two male sexual skills, important as they are, are only the beginning of what a man has to know and do to be considered a good lover.

CHAPTER 6

BIRTH CONTROL, DISEASE PRE- VENTION, AND OTHER DOWNERS

When a man loves a woman, there are some serious considerations he needs to pay attention to regarding their sexual relationship. In the past, men have often ignored these concerns or assumed that they are the woman's problem. But avoiding these sometimes unpleasant facts of life can only create bigger problems in the future, so such issues do need to be considered by a responsible and loving man.

Birth Control

A man who is not fully aware of the need for mutually responsible birth control cannot be considered a good lover.

Unless a woman is sterile or the man has a vasectomy, pregnancy is going to be a concern that he needs to participate in.

When making love, nobody wants to have to bother with jellies, conundrums, or diagrams. Practicing contraception is a drag on sexuality. Many men simply ignore the issue. The woman, left with the burden of responsibility, may just cross her fingers and hope that she is not ovulating. Or, a couple may practice half measures like *coitus interruptus* (pulling out, to you and me) or having intercourse for a while before he comes some other way.

Sometimes this method works; most often it doesn't and pregnancy follows. In the case of an unwanted pregnancy, abortion is an obvious consideration. However, even if we don't exclude women for whom abortion is morally inconceivable, terminating a pregnancy is no simple matter.

A woman may experience great discomfort and pain before, during, and after the operation. She'll lose work. She may be nauseated for weeks before and bleed for weeks after. She may have to have a second abortion because the first didn't work. She may have an ectopic (tubal) pregnancy and lose a fallopian tube after major surgery. Every one of these mishaps has happened to one or another acquaintance of mine in the last twelve months. These occurrences seem to be the rule rather than the exception.

Abortion, moreover, is a loss—no matter what you believe about when human life begins. The loss of a fetus can be a sorrowful, wrenching experience for a woman and a man. Many people experience an abortion with the same grief and mourning as a death in the family.

So, though it may be convenient for men to think of abortions as regrettable but minor inconveniences about which they need not worry, the fact is that while some are uneventful, many are not. Therefore, before making love with a woman, the only responsible course of action for a man is to have a thorough conversation with her about birth control. Besides, it is in his interest to have a confident, comfortable partner rather than one who is fearful and worried.

Has she been pregnant? What birth control does she use or prefer? Would she rather they don't have intercourse? And while they're on the subject, is she susceptible to irritations, or yeast or other infections?

This may sound dreadful. Do I really mean to suggest that in the midst of passionate escalation toward lovemaking, as zippers melt away and garments fly into the wind, we are supposed to stop and say, "Wait a minute, let's talk about birth control and herpes?" A man may feel that to get into a serious conversation at that point would obviously ruin the occasion.

"If it's a problem," you might quip, "she'll bring it up. The fact that she doesn't means everything is all right." Wrong! She probably finds the matter as embarrassing as you do. Everything may be okay, in fact, but you never know for sure, and even if it is, she will appreciate your asking. Unless she is ambivalent to begin with, your concern will endear you to her all the more. And certainly both of you should find out whether either of you has herpes or any other disease.

Let me now provide some information about which, to my surprise, I have found some otherwise clever people to be unaware:

*A woman *can* get pregnant during her period. Ovulation and menstruation are not always as separate as they are supposed to be, and a sperm can survive for days within a woman's body.

*Ejaculation is not necessary for pregnancy; intercourse without ejaculation can bring about pregnancy because of sperm-laden, pre-ejaculatory male secretions.

55

*A woman does not have to have an orgasm to get pregnant.

Male Contraception

Let us speak of rubbers and vasectomies. Provided they don't break or come off, rubbers are the most effective form of mechanical contraception. Therefore, you must know how to use them. Now, rubbers are a difficult subject for men and believe it or not, I don't feel equal to the task. Let me quote Coach Al Ellis' locker room speech to the boys of the victorious San Remo High 1985 graduating class:

"Okay men, this is a pep talk. Today I am going to tell you about rubbers and winning. Now you know that I would not send you to the showers with your socks on or that I would not ask you to get into a hot tub in your raincoats, but this, believe me, is important, and it's not so bad as you guys seem to think it is.

"The deal with rubbers is that it's all in the wrist; putting them on is what I mean. You can put on a rubber wrong, and it is going to feel like you are stirring your thing in a box of crackers, not to speak of how it is going to feel to the lady in question. But if you know how to put them on, rubbers can be almost as good as the naked item.

"So listen up. The secret of the rubber is lubrication. Now you guys know about lubrication. It's no good if it is the wrong kind or if it doesn't reach all the parts which are rubbing against each other. So, you need proper lubrication on the inside of the rubber between you and it, and on the outside between it and the lady. Between you and me, I know of no better lubricant for the inside of your rubber than your very own spit. Now, the stuff that comes with the so-called lubricated con-

56

doms is no good; it doesn't slide. Spit works, it slips and slides, and it's the best. So you get plenty of spit around the head of your member and roll the rubber all the way up to the old pubic bone. Don't lubricate the neck, because you want the rubber to stick rather than slip off during the heat of engagement.

"Okay, for the lubrication outside of your rubber the ideal, of course, is the natural lubrication of a really juicy woman. It's a really good idea not to go inside a woman until she is good and wet. But some women don't lubricate that much, even if they are super turned on, so in that scenario spit is still good. The problem is that spit has germs in it and could cause irritations and infection in the lady's vagina, so you better talk it over with her. She may want to try your spit or hers, or she may want to use some commercially available lubricant. The problem with store-bought lubricants is that some people feel they sting, and they definitely taste funny.

"Going back to putting on the rubber, you need to really lubricate the inside of it if it's going to feel good. If you have a problem with spit, maybe you have a dry mouth from breathing so hard; then water will do almost as well.

"I know, this sounds like a lot of trouble, but the point is that birth control is a necessary bother, and a considerate man will share the responsibility of it. The lady will appreciate it, I know Mrs. Ellis does.

"Now let me tell you about embarrassment. Some guys are so embarrassed about these things that they would rather just forget about them; look the other way, if you know what I mean, into her eyes, and forget what's going on down there. Some guys even lose their hard they get so embarrassed. Well, if you are going to lose your hard you better get over being embarrassed;

57

looking the other way is not, I repeat, not an option this season. It used to be that all we cared about is scoring, right? Well, scoring isn't good enough any more; we have to be thoughtful, kind, and considerate, or we'll score once and then get cut, and I don't mean maybe.

"These are the eighties, fellows, and this is America, and the word is responsibility, and we are talking about responsibility for birth control and disease prevention, and we are talking about sharing it fair and square. So get out there and learn the art of putting on those rubbers and not being embarrassed and getting it on with the lady of your choice so that she'll choose you the next time around. You can do the right thing and I know you will. Go get them."

So spoke Coach Ellis and he was right. Rubbers, provided they don't come off or break, are the most effective form of mechanical contraception. In addition, they are the only effective method to prevent contagion or disease. Unfortunately, many men seem to have a great phobia against them. Granted, intercourse is more pleasant without them. Nevertheless, that is no reason for the adamant refusal of their use by some men. To be regarded as a considerate lover a man must be able and willing to use condoms.

Vasectomy

Vasectomies are the other method of male birth control. Briefly, a vasectomy is a minor surgical procedure that takes about 15 minutes and is usually done in a doctor's office under local anesthetic. It costs about $150 to $300. The operation involves the cutting of the *vas deferens*, the tube that carries sperm from the testicles to the penis. After the tubes are cut, the loose ends are tied. In this way the sperm produced by the testes are blocked

58

and dissolve. The sperm accounts for only ten percent of a man's come, so ejaculation continues to occur. Vasectomies have no proven negative long-term effects, though considerable discomfort can occur for as long as a month after the operation.

Men's largest concern about vasectomy is that it's a sort of semicastration that will demasculinize them or worse, leave them impotent. Vern, a man who eventually obtained a vasectomy, told me of his doubts:

"I was forty-three years old and had two children. Over the last five years I had been thinking of getting a vasectomy, but somehow I was afraid that it would take away my sexuality. One thing I was afraid about is that women would think me less sexy or that it would have some kind of long-term effect. I had heard that there were suspected circulation and heart problems. But what really worried me was the loss of sexuality.

"What eventually caused me to get the operation is that I was involved in a couple of unwanted pregnancies and decided that I never again wanted to participate in the pain and heartbreak of an abortion. So I went ahead.

"I have found out that I feel as sexy as ever and that women's usual reaction when they find out about it is one of great relief and appreciation. I am really glad that I did it and have never had any regrets. In fact, every so often I forget that I am sterile so I certainly don't feel any loss of manhood."

Recently, vasectomies are being reversed, though the success rate is about 50-50 and the procedure is expensive.

Considering all the facts about male and female birth control methods, and how much more of a burden the reproductive process tends to be on the woman, it seems that when a man loves a woman, he would seriously

59

consider a vasectomy as the form of birth control in a relationship, given that he has decided that he no longer wants to have children.

When Not to Have Intercourse

There are a number of reasons why after a discussion you should not have intercourse:

*There is no birth control available.

*The birth control available is not fully satisfactory (e.g., she doesn't trust rubbers, and you don't trust diaphragms).

*One of you has an infection or irritation.

*One of you has an active case of herpes.

If for some reason you decide not to have intercourse, you must not assume you can't have sex. There are a number of delightful, mutually satisfying alternative ways to make love: cunnilingus, fellatio, and mutual masturbation. In the past, anal intercourse would have been included in a list of alternatives to genital intercourse, but recently it appears that this form of intercourse is a major way in which AIDS is spread. Consequently, caution is advised regarding anal intercourse.

With the woman on her stomach you can spill your semen on her back and then give her a massage with it. The semen will act as a vanishing cream and be completely, odorlessly absorbed into her skin, leaving it velvet smooth. Or, she can eat you until you come, not swallow, and then give you a chest or back rub with it.

This has been said a thousand times, but it bears repeating. The important aspect of making love is the full skin contact, the tenderness, the enjoyment, the ecstasies of orgasm. Whether this is achieved through intercourse or some other means is not as important as

60

ensuring that both partners are relaxed, free of anxiety, and therefore open to the fullest possible enjoyment. The insistence on intercourse as the only valid form of sexual lovemaking is an obstacle to sexual fulfillment.

Disease Prevention

Unless you both have been celibate for a long time, venereal disease has to be considered when you are about to make love to a woman for the first time. The reasons for taking responsibility to initiate this discussion are similar to the reasons for initiating the conversation about birth control: She may be concerned about it and reluctant to bring it up. So be a gentleman and deal with it.

If you have herpes, it is necessary that you mention it, even if it isn't an active case. Not mentioning it could ruin the rest of your relationship, or your reputation— not to speak of the disastrous consequences of passing it on to her. If you don't have herpes, then it's important to make sure she doesn't either, and if she does, make sure to take precautions.

Here is some information worth keeping in mind:

*Herpes lesions on the mouth can be communicated to the genitals through cunnilingus or fellatio.

*You must wash yourself thoroughly with soap and water before having intercourse with a woman if a) you have had intercourse with another woman, or if b) you have had anal intercourse. Both of these instances are likely to deposit bacteria on your penis that will multiply and could cause infection in your partner. Even if you washed once, you should wash before intercourse because over a period of time a few bugs remaining after your initial washing can proliferate.

*If a woman is prone to bladder infections, or if the

man is a lot heavier, she should be on top when having intercourse because the man-above position tends to push bacteria into her urinary tract. In any case, a woman should urinate soon after intercourse to flush out bacteria that may have been forced into her urinary tract.

*Intercourse when the woman is not lubricated can be dangerous in addition to being unpleasant. Abrasions and lesions can result, which are opportunities for infection.

Disease prevention and birth control are extremely important issues to women, and a man who takes them seriously will be greatly appreciated for his concern. When you take time to deal with these problems, you are laying the foundation for mutual respect and greater intimacy in the relationship.

CHAPTER 7

FRILLS, CHILLS,

AND THRILLS

Now that we have the downers of sex behind us, we can go on to its delights: the special treats, gourmet delicacies of thoughtful and sophisticated sexuality.

Coming Together

Everyone who's ever written about sex has a personal preference that, in some way or another, finds its way into his or her writings. Whether it be fellatio, anal or tantric sex, or what have you, a preference will be unconsciously highlighted.

To avoid this kind of embarrassment, I will confess right now that my sexual *ne plus ultra* is simultaneous orgasm.

An orgasm is a thrilling outpouring of energy. The energetic release of orgasm is pleasurable enough by itself, but when I am being bathed in another person's outpouring at the same time as my orgasm occurs, my pleasure is synergetically multiplied. What is given is returned a hundredfold, creating a dizzying maelstrom of circular motion, in which ordinary consciousness is transformed into quintessential, timeless pleasure.

Coming together requires two people who have reasonably good control over their orgasm. Whoever arrives at the edge first needs to be able to hold back while the other gets there too. Sometimes this can become a game; both partners will hold back and "ride the edge" until one can't wait any more. A friendly contest can develop to see who can bring the other to lose control.

In my experience, the best orgasms occur when, after coming to the very verge, both partners become still, moving ever so slightly, just enough to stay on that edge for minutes at a time—then deliberately let go, all at once and together, riding the roller coaster to the eventual bottom. It seems that the longer orgasm is held back the better it eventually feels. This, incidentally, need not be only through intercourse. A man can masturbate while he eats his partner. She can masturbate or he can stimulate her manually while inside her. They can both masturbate while in each other's arms, or they can even come together over the phone while in Ma Bell's cradle.

As I pointed out before, not everyone enjoys simultaneous orgasms. Some people prefer to take turns, to enjoy their own and their partner's separately. I mention it here because it's my favorite and as an additional suggestion connected with the development of ejaculatory control.

The Sounds of Love

The instinctive thing to do when making love and enjoying it is to make sounds. Unfortunately, we tend to suppress such exhibitions of joy because we are ashamed, or embarrassed, or because the walls between our bedroom and the neighbor's kitchen are paper thin. The enjoyment of sex depends a great deal on letting go; letting go of inhibitions, of physical tension, or moving, talking, and singing the praises of love. A sexual partner who lets go of his or her voice when making love can be exciting indeed.

"When I was married, my husband and I made love totally quietly. We enjoyed it all right, but I had no idea what we were missing. Then after we divorced I met this lover who the first time he came with me, scared me practically to death. I thought he was having a heart attack. After I realized that those were normal love-making sounds, and he begged me to make sounds too, my sexual experience became a whole other thing. Like the difference between a stifled little sneeze and a head-clearing, earthshaking snorter."

"With some guys, you can't tell when they are coming, you can just tell that it's all over from the way they relax. I feel cheated when that happens. At least I want to know when he is having the pleasure of orgasm. I love to be aware of the way his orgasm builds and when he lets go. I want to be right there taking it all in. The louder the better, as far as I am concerned."

It is a rare luxury, given how we are usually surrounded by people, to give full vent to the sounds of lovemaking. But it is an incomparable experience worth pursuing. Sometime when you can take your lover to a mountain or seashore far away from people, arrange to make love out in the open where you can let go of any amount of noise you might care to make. If you succeed in letting go, it may spoil your future lovemaking in situations where you have to stifle your pleasure, but at least you will know what you're missing. And if you can't find the kind of open spaces I'm rec-

65

ommending, I understand that an approximately similar effect can be achieved in the back of a pickup on a California freeway under the hot starry night sky:

"My girlfriend and I were on a double date with this other couple. We had talked about wanting to make love and having no place to do it. So we agreed to take turns trucking and fucking. First, we drove and they made love. We had the radio on full blast listening to country music and drove down the lonely highway. If a truck came close, we slowed down or speeded up so that no one could really see what was going on. Then it was our turn, and they returned the favor. The best part is that we could whoop and holler and make all the noise we wanted to make. It was great and a little scary and very exciting. Thank God for pickups, highways, country music, and good friends."

Vibrators

Men tend to be uptight about vibrators. Some of us react to them as if they represented a challenge to our manhood. "Why should she need [or enjoy] a mechanical device when she has my magnificent tool?" we ask, or

"How can I compete with a megawatt turbo-propelled gadget like that? She's going to get addicted to it and never need me again," or "It's not natural; there must be something wrong with her, the way she enjoys it."

Vibrators joined the sexual revolution with the advent of the women's movement. At first they were seen by some women as reliable and trouble-free alternatives to the hassles of sex with men. Vibrators didn't get tired; they didn't stop working or start snoring at mid-orgasm. They could be turned off at any time without protest, made no demands, and did not get you pregnant. So, in a way, men's reactions are not totally off the mark;

66

many a woman has considered dumping a troublesome man when she discovered one of these high-tech, made in Japan competitors.

However, it's quite all right to enter into a three-way relationship with a woman and her vibrator. A touch of competition can be a good thing, and the fact is that some women (not all) have a perfectly easy and fun time coming with the help of one of these little helpers when they might find it hard or impossible to do so without it.

My suggestion is that you make friends with the little bugger and bring him into the family. A vibrator can come in mighty handy at that point in lovemaking when you have tried everything, are getting a cramp, and might be tempted to give up.

"Would you like to try the vibrator, my sweet?"

"Do you mind, honeycakes?"

"Not at all, darling; why don't you go ahead, and I'll come into your sugar walls from behind?" or

"Why don't you use our little buddy, and I'll hold you in my arms?"

Either way could turn a frustrating ordeal into a rip-roaring fun time.

Conscious Conception

With all of this talk about sex, people often forget that a major function of sexuality is conception. Sexuality and the mating ritual are an instinct-driven form of reproductive behavior upon which we have elaborated a unique human activity, making love.

Love is not a prerequisite of conception, but when love is a component, the sexual experience reaches an extraordinary peak.

"We were in love. We had known each other for five

years, and loved each other before we ever had sex. When we did, it was fabulous. We both wanted to have a child, and when we finally decided to and made love without contraceptives, without fears, with complete abandon, the experience was without equal in all of my years of lovemaking."

"Our sexuality was extremely powerful with each other, and we usually came together. She usually started coming and her vaginal contractions got me off, but there was always the contraceptive, the rubber or diaphragm between us, and the anxiety of possible pregnancy, however small. But when we made love to make a baby, all the obstacles were gone. I could feel her vagina contracting and literally sucking the orgasm out of me. I could feel the streaming of my seed through my penis and she could feel it splashing against her cervix and being sucked up into her uterus. Both of us had the similar feeling of being fused into a glowing, pulsating white ball of energy, our sweet new baby. Sex is wonderful but this was more than sex; it was love, passion, and conception all in one. Never to be forgotten."

The experience of conscious, loving conception, which everyone deserves but very few have, even once, is the ultimate expression of lovemaking. When a man loves a woman, this is among the most loving acts he can perform, and if they are both made happy by its consequences, he is a lucky man indeed.

| CHAPTER 8 | WHAT WOMEN |
| | WANT FROM US |

Giving affection is an instinct upon which human beings have developed a complex, multifaceted art. While we all have the instinct, not all people are equally skilled in the art.

People's repertories are often limited; for men, love is often restricted to sexual lovemaking or fatherly concern. We are often embarrassed by the idea of an extravagant show of affection. For women, on the other hand, love tends to be connected with the open flow and expression of affection strongly felt and often quite separate from sexuality.

Men and women enjoy each other's style of loving; in fact, receiving that which we don't have to give is a special pleasure. Women enjoy men's physicality and passion; men enjoy women's tenderness and nurturing. But when we want to get back some of what we give, we often find that our opposite number is struck dumb and that there seems to be no way to get what we want and need.

Instead of giving what the other wants, we often just give more of what we want and know how to give. Consequently, we find ourselves giving more and getting less of what *we* need in return. Ultimately, men often develop the feeling that women' needs are infinite and impossible to satisfy. In fact, what women want is simple and finite, only we don't always know how to give it. Typically, men find it difficult to get the kind of sexual attention they want, and women have trouble getting the nurturing, gentle tenderness they crave.

That Cursed Roving Eye

In interviewing women for this book, the very first question we asked was, "When you first meet a man, what auses you to be interested?" The next question was, "When you first meet a man, what turns you off?"

The answer to the first question almost universally referred to the man's personality—his energy, his interests, his "vibrations." It seldom had to do with his precise physical characteristics. One of the responses that came up with a great deal of frequency had to do with the man's eyes. "How he looks at me," or "What part of me he looks at." The following are typical responses from several women.

"If he looks at me with interest, I like it."

"It's all in the eyes, the eyes are very important."

"It's the sparkle in his eye that first draws my attention."

"It's not the eyes themselves, but what they see that I care about."

On closer investigation it seems that the women who responded in this way were tuning in to the fact that when men look at women, they frequently eye them with some very precise standards having to do with their physical appearance.

Beauty is in the eye of the beholder. Unfortunately, this presents many men an immediate difficulty. Our eyes are trained to notice the physical characteristics of our environment. We are tuned in to dimensions and proportions, and this tendency carries over to our perception of women. We tend to see women's bodies before we see anything else.

Women often complain that men objectify them. The men are often puzzled by what is meant by that accusation. Women are not helpful in explaining what they are trying to say, though they seem to know clearly that it makes them uncomfortable.

"He looks at me as a sexual object," one complained.

"All he wants is sex," added another.

"He is interested in my body, not my personality," said a third one.

"I feel like a piece of meat in a butcher shop."

This type of comment is usually unfair and seldom makes any sense to men. Very rarely is it true that a man regards a woman in such a shallow and crude manner. Women are not sides of beef or mannequins in a clothes shop to us. Our hearts and senses and minds are moved by them, and we know it. Yet there is, sadly, more than a grain of truth to these accusations.

Psychologists recording the eye movements of persons looking at a painting have found that different people look at different parts of the canvas in different sequences. Some pay attention to one detail; others sweep over the whole canvas. While I know of no scientific research about what men look at when they meet women, some women have become acutely aware of what it is. Unfortunately, men's perceptions have been deeply affected by a narrow definition of female beauty that has trained the male eye so that it will almost automatically fix itself on the breasts, waist, hips, legs, and facial features. Based on a set of "acceptable" standards of appearance, men run a virtual spot evaluation:

Breasts (check one) 1. Too big.
  2. Too small.
  3. Perfect.

Legs (check one) 1. Too short.
  2. Too fat.
  3. Too skinny.
  4. Perfect.

Hips (check one) 1. Too large.
  2. Too small.
  3. Perfect.

Face (check one) 1. Ugly.
  2. So-so.
  3. Perfect.

*Add up scores
*Choose women with highest scores.

Certain of us may be more interested in breasts than hips, or in legs rather than breasts. There is a certain latitude about what is or isn't acceptable. Some men, of course, are less afflicted by this curse than others, but unfortunately, it affects far too many of us.

However, the problem is not really that men look at women's breasts, hips, and legs. Women's bodies are beautiful, so why not look at them? The problem is that we evaluate them and find them mostly wanting—we don't see the beauty that is there. In my opinion, much of what women so dislike about men's roving eye is that it judges, for the most part, unfavorably. If men just looked and appreciated more of what they saw, their gaze would lose the hungry or rejecting edge and be less offensive.

This type of appraisal is not the exclusive domain of men. Women have looked at men with precise standards in mind as well—mostly having to do with men's power, their ability to be providers and protectors. At times their checklist is as cold-blooded as men's, from make, model, and year of his car to gross adjusted income. To the accusation "Men look at women as sex objects," men can respond, "Women look at men as money objects." Both are exaggerated caricatures, but both have some truth to them.

Women also have their own physical preferences, such as size, age, legs, face, shoulders, or waist. A *Village Voice* poll, for instance, found eyes to be highest ranking, while asses came in second.

But—and this is very important—most women questioned made it clear that physical attributes aren't the most important. Much more often mentioned were, "a sexy mind," "tone of voice," "intelligence and charm," "attitude," "level of energy," "a man who pays attention to me," "the way he stands," "a passionate man," and over and over, his eyes. In other words, women do tend to see more of the whole person.

While some women find men's fixation on their bodies flattering, many women, especially women who think of themselves as intelligent, powerful, interesting, or independent, find it insulting. But when a man looks

73

at the whole woman with interest, if he looks at her eyes, at her face, at her hands, at her whole body rather than her body parts, then she will take note as well, and do so with appreciation.

Men's difficulty in seeing beyond the very physical characteristics of women is one of the reasons why they have difficulty giving women what they want. Clearly, it won't do for a man, upon meeting a woman, to say, "I am fascinated by your beautiful breasts," or "I find your legs most attractive." That is probably not what she wants to hear. If that is all he sees, he had better remain silent lest he be judged a Neanderthal pig. And if he sees nothing at all that pleases him, he's in even worse trouble since his eyes will usually reveal that fact to a perceptive woman.

One of the reasons why we men focus on visual factors has to do with our egos; our need for self-esteem and prestige. We fantasize being seen with a woman walking into a party, driving down the street with her in a convertible, sitting at a restaurant table, or walking down the aisle. We imagine other men appraise her and approve of her as a woman they'd like to be with, a woman they would compete for. Or we imagine that other men will find her ugly and lose respect for us for being seen with her.

There is nothing wrong with wanting to be with someone that we like and that others will like as well. But we have to ask ourselves whether we want to let other people's visual standards guide our lives. True, certain women will rouse envy and admiration in men. So will a shiny new car or a yacht. In the very short run there is nothing like a gorgeous woman on one's arm to attract people's attention and give us prestige. But be-

74

yond the short run it isn't just looks, but everything else that makes people attractive. Just as desirable is being with someone who is alive, happy, and full of love.

Bruce, a successful writer in his 40's who had been married twice, said: "I picked my first wife out of a crowd, at a literary party. Within minutes of meeting her I knew I wanted to marry her. Actually, making her mine would be a more exact expression of how I thought of it. Everyone thought she was a stunning beauty and a fitting companion to a young, up-and-coming writer like myself. Well, she was good-looking, no doubt, but our relationship was completely based on her looks and my success. When we were alone with each other we were quite simply bored. My second wife and I were not attracted to each other at first; we just did not fit each other's idea of what each other should be. But we liked each other more and more, rather quickly. Men don't do double takes over her on the street, but my friends love her and love to hang out with us."

Women, too, get caught in this kind of a trap. To be seen with a rich powerful man will arouse envy and admiration, and will cause women to overlook their more intimate needs in favor of social flattery. How often has a woman picked a silent, powerful man and discovered too late that he is cold and ungiving?

When people pick their partners on such superficial bases, they must expect that their choices will be potentially flawed. In time, the more important, more mutually satisfying dimensions of the person may turn out to be absent. Long after the crowds give their approval, we have to deal with our choice's true personality and may find it wanting.

EXERCISE ONE: RETRAINING THE EYE

So it is important to retrain the eye. But how can we alter this perverse, seemingly irresistible tendency? There is something we can do to modify the way in which we perceive women so that when we first meet them, our eyes actually see beyond their physical characteristics and into the many other dimensions of their person.

When meeting a woman it's a good idea to disregard our strong tendency to pay attention to her superficial dimensions. If our objectifying eye focuses on some "blemish," it's very effective to overlook that unattractive flaw and search instead for something we find pleasing. If the eye is attracted to a nose that doesn't have the exact perfect width, length, or turn, then we consciously look for something that we like that does not have to do with her breasts, hips, or legs such as her eyes, her hands, how proudly she stands. We can take note of what we like and go on to other, more psychological, aspects of her person; her attitude, her intelligence or creativity. On the other hand, when we meet a woman who is a media beauty, a "10," we need to overlook her irresistible "perfect" features and look for other things again; her hands, her voice, what she does and likes, who she is.

That is, in fact, what women seem to do when they consider men. One woman says:

"Soon after I meet a man, if I am going to like him, I know what part of him is going to attract me. His smell, his hands, his voice, the way he stands, his arms. That's what I am drawn to over and over."

Another woman says:

"Nobody is perfect. When I like a man, I am drawn

to some feature of his. It can be anything—I'm not choosy—like his profile or his skin. Other things don't seem to matter much."

Years ago I simply could not see beyond women's body parts. My friends could predict ahead of time which women I would be interested in and which women I would ignore. I was repeatedly and severely criticized for this behavior.

In addition, only a few women were flawless enough for me to be interested. Usually, these women were the focus of many other men's interest as well, and I found that there was usually some other dude who was more attractive to them then I. So, the beauty, more often than not, left me in the dust as she and this other fellow walked hand in hand into the sunset.

When I realized, in desperation, how harmful was my affliction, I began to retrain my eye. I practiced for several months until it became second nature. I tamed my eye's automatic scanning of breasts, hips, legs. I refused to reexamine the aspects of a woman that I found unpleasing. I forced myself to go on from the easily perceived to the more subtle. I searched for un-noticed beauty, explored it, and expanded my aware-ness. I discovered how much unseen perfection, how much power, sparkle, intelligence, and sweetness there is in people after I looked beyond my eye's first focus. When I found something I liked, I rested on it, relished and savored it.

One glorious spring morning I noticed an unusually large number of beautiful women walking the streets of Berkeley. I was puzzled. Was there a women's conven-tion in town, or perhaps a new influx of coeds at the university? Was spring forcing all the beautiful women into the streets? But no, the women hadn't changed. It was me. My eyes were seeing beautiful flowing hair, ample hips, strong legs, faces full of character, self-assured gaits. And, as I let myself admire these lovely things, I saw shining eyes returning the compliment with a smile and a flick of the shoulder that signaled their appreciation.

Since then, though not completely cured, I am definitely much improved. The world is full of beautiful women; too many in fact to fully attend to. I am like a kid in a candy store—all due to a simple (though not so easy) change in perception stimulated by retraining the eye.

The eyes are the window of the soul, or so it is said. Eye contact is a very important aspect of first meeting a person. We often avoid eye contact because we're afraid of what we might see and of being seen. When looking into each other's eyes, people connect in a way that has nothing to do with any other physical attribute; attention flows directly between them without getting hung up on this or that superficial detail. If the eye contact is accompanied by a handshake, a closed circuit of energy flow is established that can say a great deal about what is happening between the people involved. Whether the two people are compatible and will like each other enough to pursue each other's friendship is often decided in the first few seconds of contact.

This kind of eye and hand encounter will leave you with a number of impressions when you meet a woman. Only if you are able to see beyond the surface, will the way you see her, please her. Once you discover what delights you about her, you are well on your way to phrasing your appreciation in a manner that will feel good to her.

So exercise one is retraining the eye and finding the

beauty. To practice it go somewhere where you can sit unobtrusively and observe many people, like a beach, a shopping mall, or a busy street. Observe ordinary people as they go by, not "10's" but "4's" and "5's." Search for something which is pleasing to you. Refuse to dwell on what you don't like.

Next, spend time with a woman you know casually. Once again search for positive attributes, this time psychological attributes: her attitude, her creativity, her intelligence, her energy, what have you. And don't focus on what you don't appreciate.

Get the idea? Okay then, practice, practice, practice.

EXERCISE TWO: TALK TO ME SWEETLY.

Once we have found what it is we like about another person, we can proceed to say it. For some people this is an easy task. But for others actually saying what they like and how they like it is quite difficult. They become tongue-tied with apprehension.

"What if she hates what I say?"

"What if I make a fool of myself? I'm not good with words."

The heart beats faster, and he starts to sweat. "Maybe I should wait; tomorrow is another day."

"She knows I like her; why repeat the obvious?"

One of the reasons men don't express their appreciation to women is that often men feel that such a confession is tantamount to making a commitment. "If I tell her how beautiful she is to me, she'll think I'm in love, and she'll expect me to marry her and I'll have to buy a house and two cars and I'll have to support her and the kids, forever." A man who is fleeing commitment will be especially reluctant to say how much he likes a woman because to do so cuts off his escape path, or so he fears. No wonder he breaks out in a cold sweat!

Telling someone how much we appreciate her doesn't automatically signal lifelong commitment. Strokes and compliments can be given freely without fear of the "tender trap." However, it is true that because some women find the experience of receiving heartfelt strokes from men quite unusual, there is room for potential misunderstanding here. A woman may, in fact, wrongly interpret this experience. Still it seems better to be loving and then deal with any possible misunderstanding than not to love at all.

In any case, if we are worried about how people are going to take our compliments, it's a good idea to prepare them by "paving the way":

"I have been noticing you the last few minutes; may I give you a compliment?" or,

"Can I tell you something I like about you?" or,

"I don't know you, but would you be offended if I told you something that struck me as very attractive about you?" or,

"I am wanting to tell you something, but I'm worried. Can I explain what I am feeling?"

At this point you have perceived something you like about a woman and have made sure that she is willing to hear your compliment and to hear it as you mean it. It's time to put it into words.

A compliment doesn't have to pass muster as scientific truth. But it has to come from the heart—it needs to be sincere. If I say, "I think you are beautiful (smart, funny)," I only have to make sure that I truly believe it. Even though it is important to generate warm appreciation where there may initially be lukewarm interest, it is absolutely essential that it be heartfelt rather than a white lie. Once you have figured out what you sincerely like about a person, it won't hurt to go somewhat overboard and be biased, hyperbolical, and metaphoric, particularly since men tend to be objective, laconic, and sparse. In other words, when it comes to compliments, it's better to go slightly overboard than to fall short. It's better to be melodic, rhapsodic, or poetic than to be boring.

For instance, if you are inclined to say, "You are smart," why not say, "I have been noticing you talking to different people and realized how really smart you are"? Instead of saying, "You are funny," why not say, "You know something, you really crack me up. I love your sense of humor"? Why say, "You are beautiful," when you can say, "Every so often when I look at you, I am startled by your beauty. Sometimes you take my breath away"?

And of course, nothing is as well received as when at a chosen moment we catch the attention of someone we love and sincerely, smilingly, unhesitatingly recite the shortest, sweetest poem of all: "I love you." Women like poetry so let every affectionate statement be a poem.

As you begin to express your affection, some women may mistrust you and not believe it. A woman may shrug imperceptibly, or make a face or blink or close her eyes while she listens internally to a voice saying, "Oh, he is just saying that to make you feel good," or "Oh, oh, here comes the sexual pitch."

If you suspect that kind of thing you can ask, "Did you hear what I just said?" "Did you believe it?"

She may answer, "You don't really mean that; you are just saying it." You will be able to answer, convincingly, "But I do, I really, truly do." Try again and ask her to believe you this time.

On the other hand she may respond with a toothsome

smile, a hug, or a happy sigh, and then you'll know that you have successfully engaged in a reciprocal, if small, loving act—the giving and taking of affection.

So, exercise two is talk to me sweetly (and watch me melt). To practice this exercise start by choosing a person you know and can trust and after asking her for permission tell her some of the flattering thoughts you have had about her. After you can do this easily, practice on people you don't know well; at work, school, or in the street.

EXERCISE THREE: LOVE ME BEYOND WORDS.

So far, I have been referring exclusively to the verbal expression of positive feelings. But there are other ways in which people show their love. For instance, the very fact that two people are having a good conversation, even if it does not include overt statements of affection, is a form of mutual appreciation. In the process of a conversation, a person responds positively to another by listening, carefully considering what the other is saying, and taking it seriously, by either agreeing or respectfully disagreeing and by showing recognition of what is being said by nodding, smiling, or even laughing.

One of the subtle aspects of verbal communication is the tonality of the voice, which expresses the emotional content behind what one is saying. The very same word, spoken with different tones of voice, can have widely different meanings. Obviously, a gentle, tender tone of voice is going to heighten the positive effects of a statement, compared to a flat or harsh one. Even if all meaning is extracted from somebody's speech, it's usually clear to a listener whether the speaker is expressing a positive, neutral, or negative attitude just from the tone of it.

How something is said as well as *what* is said is, therefore, a very important aspect of what a man desiring to become a loving person needs to pay attention to. Practice tender speech; if you have difficulty speaking softly and lovingly to a person, practice with a kitten, or a baby.

At times women don't seem to want to be touched by men, and the reason is that they fear that if they accept a man's touch, it will be interpreted as sexual acquiescence.

Women may seem overly paranoid in this respect, but men consistently interpret friendliness and openness on the part of women as a sexual invitation. This is something that women have come to resent. Some have come to absolutely hate it.

"Why can't he touch me without immediately getting turned on and wanting sex?" one asked.

"Unless I know I want sex with a man, I don't dare let him touch me because he'll think it's a come-on," said another.

Yet another swore, "I won't touch a man unless I know I want to have sex with him."

Closely related to the sexual touch is the power touch. Men often touch women as a way to assert their manhood, their control and power. We hold a woman's elbow; we take their hands in ours, guide them through doors or down the street. All this can be innocent enough, but often it's a way to show mastery and then it is resented.

So men who are shy about touching women have good reason. Men as a rule don't have an accurate grasp

83

of the extent to which they invade women's privacy. Men are allowed to own the space they occupy and to move aggressively out of it into other people's—especially women's. A man who is sensitive recognizes that in almost any situation involving women he has the potential of a bull in a china shop. To take the risk of touching them without creating problems requires a certain amount of sensitivity.

The hands are most naturally extensions of the heart. They are the ideal instruments of love. Men seldom use their hands for any purpose other than sexuality or manipulation. Many men touch children, or other men, or women only when they want to control them. The benefits of touching are largely inaccessible to these men; consequently, they don't touch as much as they need to, and tend to be underdeveloped in the gentle art of touching. Yet, men's hands are often strong and skilled in other ways, and it would not take much to learn their loving, pleasure-giving capacities.

The sensitive touch combines love and intuition. Love provides the energy, and intuition gives us the knowledge of how to best direct our energy to soothe and give pleasure. With our intuition, we can sense other people's need for touch.

If we pay attention, we will notice when people have backaches, when they are in need of encouragement and support, or when they just want to be touched. This intuitive awareness, combined with a loving energy, is the basis for the loving touch.

Opportunities to touch will present themselves if you are seeking them. People will complain of headaches, pain in the back, sore feet, tired hands, all of which can be soothed with touch. There is, of course, the initial touch of the handshake. Beyond that, it is possible to

84

touch people while speaking to them, while taking walks, while going past them in close quarters, and when bidding them goodbye. Brushing someone's hair can help a headache; holding and massaging someone's hand can relieve their tension.

All sorts of possibilities for touch are available and should be considered by a man who wants to become more loving. The essential task, however, is to touch regardless of any sexual considerations—to touch without expecting sexuality to become an aspect of the touching. That will mean that we will touch without discrimination; we will touch those we are attracted to as much as those we do not find sexually attractive.

One very good way of becoming acquainted with the way in which our hands can impart pleasure is to learn massage. Any man who wants to become more loving can take a massage course and find opportunities to practice on people he is close to. Offer to give a head, neck, back, or foot rub. A friend may have been crying, or may have been hammering nails all day; another may have sat all day at a desk or played a hard ball game. In any one of these situations, it is possible to offer a rub as a way to show our appreciation and to practice loving others.

So, exercise three is love me beyond words (and I'll believe everything you say). Next time you have an opportunity to give someone affection, pay attention to your tone of voice, your posture, your attitude, how your feelings are transmitted through your face and, in particular, your eyes. Use your hands with people you know well; then experiment with the use of your hands with people you are not well acquainted with.

These are some of the things women want—don't treat me like a hunk of meat, talk to me sweetly, but love me beyond words. But love of women goes beyond some of these important manifestations of affection. If there is to be peace between the sexes, we need to deal with much more, as we shall see in the following chapter.

CHAPTER 9 | MAKING PEACE

BETWEEN

THE SEXES

Single men often see themselves as hunted animals, wanted by women as "meal tickets." Once trapped into marriage, they fear that they will have to provide for the woman for the rest of their lives.

On the other hand, men see women as having something they want: love, warmth, sex—which they see women using to tantalize them, and which women are not always willing to share. Given the constantly raging "war of the sexes," it is sometimes difficult for men to see women as people they can love. Though a man may be attracted to a specific woman and pursue her with the purpose of "making love," men often are deeply, simultaneously misogynists (woman haters), as evidenced by the high incidence of abuse, battering, and rape that women suffer at the hands of men.

Often, men believe they have reason to fear and be angry at women because of specific past experiences in their lives. The folklore is replete with images of women who hurt men. Men feel they are often treated unkindly by women. Women reject them or cling to them, use them, and make unreasonable demands. Many men rarely get satisfaction from women, and when they do, the satisfaction seldom lasts and often has many "strings" attached. Above all, men often feel terrorized by women's emotions, which they don't understand and can't seem to control.

Nothing will be gained by denying that women deserve anger from men. Women's role in the past required them to be passive, to get from men what they needed through devious means, and indeed, there are women who will do anything to make a man take care of them. Women, too, have been angry, often very angry, and have taken pleasure in humiliating men, making them crawl and beg for what they want. To men who are seeking a partner to share their lives, such women are the source of legitimate fear and anger.

"I'll never forget what my father once said to me," a man remembers. "He was talking about women, and he said: 'Your average woman sits on her butt waiting for a man to come along, and when one gets close enough she reaches up, grabs his balls, and hangs on for the rest of his life.' That nasty little comment has stuck with me all of these years. I don't trust women to be self-sufficient."

The strange contradiction in men's lives—their misogynous fear of women on the one hand, and their constant pursuit of women on the other—might seem irreconcilable. But it isn't if one realizes that men's anger at women comes from the frustration caused by the continual failure to get what they desperately need—emotional nourishment. In other words, men need women because we don't know how to love ourselves or others. We need women to fulfill our deep hunger for love. And when we don't succeed in stilling this hunger, we blame women and are angry at them.

Love of Women

Most women today understand the value of asking for their rights and standing up for and loving themselves. But why should men join women in their struggle for self-respect? Why should they give up their privilege— as the head of the household, having the first and last word, being able to sit at the head of the table while someone else does the dishes, having the right to take the lead in relationships, being in control? What would be left? What would men get in return? Would they find themselves one-down to women with all their new-found energies and ambition, their wondrous sexuality, their child-bearing capacities, and their magical, emotional powers?

In her book *Sex for Women*, Carmen Kerr defines feminism as "love of women." People's reactions to this definition vary. For me it was a bulls-eye; yet many people initially react to it with dislike and disagreement. Some mistrust it because it is too simple; others interpret "love of women" to mean lesbianism or simply sexuality with women. Yet, when given some thought the definition takes on meaning and validity. Love of women does not necessarily imply sexuality, nor does it exclude it. Love here refers to the whole range of positive emotions between people, from fondness to passionate sexuality.

However else the women's movement may be defined, love of women must be an important aspect of it. If women were loved as they deserve, they would be treated equitably at work. If women were loved, there would be no questions as to their rights to choose to

89

have a child or not to have it when pregnant, or to have a child whether they be single, married, or living with another person, man or woman. Love of women also requires that we account for, and be tolerant of, their cyclical, hormonal changes and the way those changes affect them—their moods and their stamina. When women are angry, love of women requires that their anger be given room for full expression. When women withdraw their love or sexuality, love of women requires that their world view be given consideration. Love of women would require great concern and active work to reverse the feminization of poverty, that devastating process that is pushing women and children to the very bottom of the economic heap. Love of women means concern for the child-related issues that affect them: child care, equal pay, pre- and post-natal medical care and pediatric services free or at greatly reduced prices when needed.

And finally, when women, as they gain power, fall into the same errors of which they have been the victims, love of women requires that they be criticized evenhandedly, without condescension or self-righteous anger, that they be given the same allowances for error we give men.

Love of women as a group, whether they be old or young, thin or fat, tall or short, regardless of their beauty, is the opposite of misogyny—the suspicion, dislike, fear, and lack of empathy for women that so afflict many men.

Hatred of men, on the other hand, is widely associated with feminism. While this is incorrect, many of us have been exposed to women (and men) who call themselves feminists and hate men.

The love of women is not served by contempt or hatred

of men, although it requires that such feelings be allowed expression and acknowledgment when they exist. On the other hand, the awe of women, which afflicts some, is also inappropriate love of women, since such extreme adoration can only lead to disappointment and eventual anger. Both women and men are human, subject to error and improvement. Both men and women are capable of being cruel and abusive. As women get power, it's becoming clear that they can be thoughtless and cruel, just like men.

But love of women also requires that people recognize one vital fact: Women have been treated badly and continue to be treated badly in comparison to men. True, both men and women have suffered. But women have had all the suffering that has been meted out to men; plus, they've suffered because they are women—suffering that remains generally unchanged throughout the world, except occasionally in a few places like middle- and upper-class North America.

Without understanding the historical fact of women's oppression and how women have learned to react to power abuse, it's not possible to appreciate women's condition and respond to it lovingly. Without knowledge of women's and men's histories as separate people, the mysteries of the love (and hate) between them cannot ever be fully understood, and the war between the sexes will continue unabated.

So why, let us ask again, should men embrace the love of women? The answer is that because in doing so we'll be handed back our hearts. Because in learning to love women, we will reclaim our loving capacities. Because if we learn to love women, we will learn to love ourselves, and each other.

In the short run, as men learn the love of women,

they'll experience love by women in return. Every feminist step that a man takes is likely to bring about some recognition and appreciation from the women around him. As he learns emotional literacy, he will reap the pleasures of improved understanding and communication between himself and the women (and men) in his life. As he honors and expresses his own feelings, he will find widening acceptance and comfort. He will gradually learn what love is really all about. He will wear his heart on his sleeve, and he will discover the well-being and joy love can bring. Love of women will also, by opening our hearts, make us more open and available to other men and their friendship.

Affection between men will be more commonplace and will not have to wait for its traditional forms of expression in the battlefield, in the sports arena, or when we get drunk together. Men will be able to love each other as they love their women friends, thereby becoming more secure about each other's affections.

And if this is not enough, in the long run, love of women will extend our lifespan by relieving us of the burden of undue financial and emotional responsibility for women and by soothing our hearts as women reciprocate our love for them. Feminism will bring us the love of our children and the respect of our co-workers, those whom we work for, and those who work for us.

As love of women increases its scope across the land and the world, it will promote women in places of power—women who are not just female replicas of heartless men, but women whose hearts will tend to humanize business, politics, religion, and all aspects of human life. With women participating in the major decisions that affect people—with women holding up half the sky—rationality will be tempered with feeling, and that cannot but benefit us all.

The issue of men's love for women goes to the core of the final section of this book. Love of women is both an outcome and a requisite for emotional development, because in learning emotional literacy we are establishing a loving relationship with, rather than rejecting, the feminine in ourselves.

The ability to nurture, to be tender and loving, the ability, in short, to feel has been women's realm. Now women are asking men to be partners with them in both the burdens and benefits of emotional aliveness. Let us, therefore, embrace the task of reclaiming and fully owning our feelings, and of learning emotional literacy.

CHAPTER 10 | FEELINGS?

Women, whether young or old, North American, Latin American, or European, whether working class, leisure class, or poor, whether women of color or white—when asked what they want from men, concentrate on a similar theme.

"Let go, give up control."

"Give of yourself."

"Listen to me, and tell me what's going on with you."

"Tell me if you love me, or if you hate me."

"Relax, find the soft part of you."

"What I feel counts; I want you to care about it."

"I want to know how you feel."

At first, these answers appear to be typical of the vague way in which women talk to men when they want something they're not getting. But in looking over these responses, I begin to see a pattern.

"Give, open up, feel, tell me, listen, be yourself"; the common thread that I detected in all these answers was

94

that women want men to become more conscious of how they feel and how women feel. And women want men to begin acting upon feelings more than they do.

"Feelings?" we are apt to respond. "What do you mean by feelings?" We are often truly puzzled by such a request. Men's reaction is an honest expression of apprehension, puzzlement, and concern. The fact that our response is often tinged with defensiveness is understandable, since we recognize the importance of the question and our problem answering it.

Feelings? To men the very word brings on a panic reaction, since past experience often indicates there may be a deep, mysterious, perhaps congenital, defect here. It's not unlike a person who suddenly finds himself on a high dive platform being encouraged to jump. "What do I do?" a man gasps to himself, hoping somebody out there can explain what this feeling thing is all about, how it functions, and how to do it without a painful belly flop and subsequent drowning.

Often this panic is compounded with resentment. "What now?" he grumbles. "First, she wanted to get married, so I did. Then she quit her job, so now I work weekends. Next she got pregnant, so we stopped having sex." By this time he is sore. "Now she wants feelings? What next?" For many men the question still remains, "What do women mean when they say they want feelings?"

It isn't as if women as a whole are particularly good at explaining men's deficiency:

"You know perfectly well what I mean. Just answer the question, 'Do you love me?' "

Or when a woman, giving way to hurt and disappointment, breaks down and cries, and he reaches out in an amorous way—she does not help matters by blubbering, without explanation: "Don't touch me! All you think about is sex!"

She may be right, since often a woman in distress seems to stimulate an unwanted male hormonal response. But he is none the wiser about what upsets her.

Certainly there is no reason why men, or women for that matter, should be able to speak fluently about feelings. Feelings are not generally discussed or consciously taught anywhere. You can't take a course on emotional literacy in college. Yet even though knowledge about feelings is not overtly taught to children, many women do pass down to their daughters the "how to's" of emotional life.

Some families and cultures allow boys more options than others, but the vast majority of males are raised within a system of attitudes that trains them to be in control of themselves and others. Out of the rainbow of emotional hues and intensities, men are traditionally allowed to express only feelings of anger (if it's righteous), guilt (if it's the result of irresponsibility), and occasionally, love (if it's new or unrequited). The subtler expressions of anger, love, guilt, or other negative emotions such as hurt, embarrassment, shame, and sadness or even positive emotions like tenderness, joy, or hope are not encouraged. Males are usually not given encouragement to have such feelings nor to talk about them if they do.

This creates the emotional gap that separates men from women. Women cry out for more feelings from men, who do not know how to respond, even if willing. Meanwhile, women don't know how to teach men or even adequately explain what they want. Women may

96

be more emotionally literate than men, but both men and women have much to learn.

The hottest controversy between the sexes by far rages over two major areas of emotion—love, sex, love and sex, love or sex. Women seem to be saying "more love" and (it appears to men) "less sex." Men seem to be saying "more sex" and (it appears to women) "less love." Ideally, everyone wants both and is getting precious little of either. Millions of words in songs, books, magazines, articles, and church sermons have been written about this issue; here is my own point of view.

Sexuality

Sexuality is a powerful, assertive emotion. Sexual feelings are most strongly felt in the genitals, but sexuality can be felt more subtly over the entire body.

"It feels like I have bubbly champagne in my legs and arms."

"Sometimes it feels like I am lying in a very swift stream and the water is flowing through me."

"It feels like lying in the hot sun on a cool spring day."

"It is intense, shaking pleasure, sometimes unbearably so."

Wherever sexuality is felt, there is often an intense sense of urgency about it. After all, a major function of sexuality is procreation. Were it not so vital to us, we might be extinct by now. Sexuality is part of a drive, an instinctive and sometimes overwhelming imperative, which, if not satisfied, can become an obsession invading all of our waking (and dreaming) life. When sexual energy doesn't find genital expression, it will find some other outlet, as Freud discovered. Sexuality is inescap-

97

able and will not be denied; it will propel human beings one way or another. If it isn't expressed through genital activity and orgasm, sexual energy can travel through unseen psychic channels to surface, eventually, in the form of aggression. It can fuel intellectual or athletic pursuit. It can create paralyzing symptoms. However sexuality eventually finds expression, it will have its day.

Sexuality transforms people. It's able to turn stable and predictable situations on their head. It is the stimulus for mixing people who might never find each other were it not for sexual propulsion. Sexuality breaks through class, race, age, and color barriers.

Sexuality is like the ladle in the soup of human life. There is nothing that stirs the pot quite like sexuality. It is a revolutionary force rivaled only by violence in its capacity to attract or repel people. Sexuality can be constructive, as in the attraction that men and women can feel for each other. Then it is a renewing, recreating life force. Or it can be destructive, as when it becomes an obsession displacing all other interests.

We are aware that emotions like anger, fear, and sexuality are intimately associated with bodily functions. This is true of all emotions, which are set apart from thoughts by this very fact. Strong emotions can produce physical symptoms such as dry mouth, dilated or constricted pupils, tears, goose bumps, heart palpitations, or trembling.

Sexuality, in particular, has strong bodily manifestations. Given full expression, sexuality is wet. Sexuality is fluid; blood, sweat, tears, spit, seminal fluids, vaginal secretions, menstrual flow, and amniotic fluid are part and parcel of the sexual experience. Some people ex-

98

perience this as messy or even disgusting and are repulsed by sexuality in its full expression.

In addition, people are often both attracted and repulsed by sexuality because it's a form of energy that radiates from people in perceptible manifestations. A person who is charged with sexuality will be palpably energized. Anyone in his or her vicinity will feel the "vibes" and be either attracted or repelled, according to their own orientation. For those favorably inclined to another's sexual energy, the experience will be positive, even a "turn on." For those not so impressed, it will be uncomfortable, even nauseating.

The fluidity of sex is not only in its moisture; sexual motions are liquid. Orgasms are like waves; sex is like a stream, like a bottomless ocean; sexual energy washes over us. The liquid nature of sexuality has to be kept in mind to understand it. Sexuality is an emotion which, like the water that makes up 90 percent of our bodies, permeates our being. When we attempt to reduce it to a mere function between genitals or a plain procreative act, we lose sight of how all-encompassing it is. When we lose awareness of our sexuality, we live at the mercy of its vagaries; we are defeated by it when we could be energized, propelled, delighted, and inspired.

Because sexuality is such a powerful emotion, there is an equally powerful, culture-wide attempt to control and curb it. People attempt to defuse sexuality by sanitizing, deodorizing, civilizing, and reducing it to a product to be sold at drugstore counters right along with condoms, contraceptive jellies, and porno magazines.

Another major method of control is through emotions like guilt and fear, often strongly associated with sexuality and its expression. Sexuality on one hand and

99

guilt and fear on the other intensely oppose each other in a paralyzing confrontation. Under their opposing influence, people freeze and dry up, sexually.

But because sexuality is such a strong feeling, it breaks through the suppression to which many men subject their emotions. Consequently, men are well acquainted with it. Starting in adolescence, when it seems to suddenly burst forth, sexuality is our emotion most in need of being handled. It usually remains so for the rest of our days, even when it seems to have temporarily disappeared from our lives and for all intents and purposes no longer affects us (or so we think).

Being "In Love"

Nearly equal to sexuality in its intensity and, therefore, in its capacity to break through male reluctance to feel is the state of being "in love." Being in love and simply loving are two different emotional experiences. The former is much more powerful than the latter, yet both are definitely related. Being in love is a condition of altered consciousness, based probably on a hormonal change of body chemistry that is sought after for its beauty, and feared for its potential to hurt us. Akin to a protracted drug experience, it has been diagnosed by cynical observers of the human condition as a state of temporary insanity. When in love, one's being resides within the loving experience; one is both blind and all-seeing, and the loving feeling colors everything with its glow.

When in love, a man's perception of his loved one is heightened and distorted as in a strange but wonderful dream. She is like a blip on a radar screen. We track her as she moves around the universe, and our heart skips a beat when she drops back into view. Her touch sends electric streams through us, converging on our heart and swelling it with feeling. And we are constantly struck by this or that flash of loveliness, glittering like the facet of a diamond.

Being in love is madness, a magnifying glass, a kaleidoscope, a cold shower, a piercing arrow, a plunge from a high rock into a deep river, soaring through the air with eyes closed.

Being in love is, in all probability, a state in which love and sexuality are commingled in one powerful experience that literally blows people's minds. It is when we are in love that "sexual chemistry" is often most obvious. Our insides melt; we see strange lights and auras; the other's smells are utterly delicious—musk, pine needles, oranges, fresh cut straw.

People who are in love are aliens among ordinary people, alternately wonderful and irritating in their ecstatic behavior. One can only wait patiently until the inevitable return from paradise brings them back to their senses. When they do—usually between six months and two years later—they will, hopefully, love each other. But often they don't, which seems to show that being in love is not just an intense case of loving. Often people who were recently in love don't seem to love each other at all but rather dislike each other, sometimes a lot. All of which seems to confirm the theory that people in love are temporarily out of their minds.

Should we avoid "falling in love" because of its obvious pitfalls? It seems many people do—men, more often than not. We fear the radical loss of control, the vulnerability, the way in which it interrupts our assigned tasks. Yet no man's emotional life is complete until he has fallen deeply in love and, some would argue, until he has had his heart broken. Only then will he know the loving experience intimately enough to be able to love adequately the next time around.

Love

Contrasted with the physical, perhaps biochemical nature of sexual and "in love" experiences, plain, regular, long-term love pales by comparison. Yet, such love is considered by some to be the most powerful force in the world. Its power has to do with its enduring, widely ranging nature.

According to medical science, the heart is a muscle that pumps blood. But the heart is also the bodily focus of love. That the heart has a connection with love seems to be generally known by poets, and lovers. This knowledge is based on the fact that we "feel" love in our hearts and breasts. But again, as is the case with sexuality— where the source is not just the penis or the clitoris— it is the whole area of the chest that is the source of love's energy; in fact, love can be felt all over the body.

Love is a subject of universal interest and fascination, probably because everyone wants to be loved and most of us feel that we aren't. Most people want a reciprocated, lasting love with another person, and that is difficult to achieve. One important reason is that we are not taught how to love except by example, and the examples we have available aren't always very good. Another reason is that love is powerful enough to frighten people, because love is a long-term, binding energy. Once we let ourselves love people, we are tied to them, to their needs, to their suffering, to their lives and deaths. To love others is to ache when they hurt, to tremble when they are afraid, to succumb when they die. It is impossible to ignore the hunger and pain of the ones we love, so we sometimes cut ourselves off from them lest their pain and need become ours. The commitment for long-lasting love frightens us and gives us pause.

Another reason why we find ourselves unable to love is that the free exchange of love is severely curtailed in our everyday lives by a series of restrictive rules we all follow to some extent—the Stroke Economy. (I discussed the theory of the Stroke Economy in my book *Scripts People Live*.) Suffice it to say here that the free exchange of affection or strokes—whether between strangers, friends, siblings, parents and their children, men and men, women and women, women and men, or the young and the old—is constantly squelched by internal inhibitions and external prohibitions against giving, asking for, and accepting love. Our natural tendencies to love and be loved need to be liberated from these restrictions by conscious efforts to exercise our loving nature such as those outlined in Chapter Eight of this book.

Love needs to be distinguished from sexuality—especially by men, for whom sex as a force often overshadows love. While love waxes or wanes slowly and steadily, sexual feelings fluctuate more frequently and powerfully. We are much more aware of the rise and fall of sexual feelings than of our changes of heart. Women tend to express their sexuality linked with love, while their love is not necessarily linked with sexuality. Men, on the other hand, tend to link their love with sexuality, while their sexuality is not necessarily linked with love. In other words, men can have sex without love more easily than women, while women can have love without sex more easily than men. This explains women's common complaints when they have sex with a man and fall in love with him, and he doesn't return the favor. Men need to know but not feel bad about this—it's simply an indication that love and sex are separate and distinct feelings, that one can happen without the other, and that men are different from women. The problem, when it becomes a problem, is due to the differences between what men and women want.

If the rise and fall of sexuality is compared with the waves in the ocean, then love is the tide. Each wave brings with it a subtle increase or decrease of the tide. Each wave comes and goes with an impressive roar, but the tide moves slowly, imperceptibly. Similarly, our loving feelings for people move slowly; it takes time to love someone fully, and it takes time to lose the loving feeling. Love, like sex, is felt as fluid, but it is experienced more as a liquid that fills, brims over, or is sadly dried up. When it flows, it flows easily, as if down a gentle hill; it swirls in the chest and floods the mind with tender, nurturing thoughts.

While the sexual and "in love" feeling can develop overnight, the experience of loving someone builds upon the shared experiences, ups and downs, deaths, births; the accumulated significant moments of being together over time. Likewise it can be destroyed through time; eroded away by large and small cruelties, misunderstandings, and luckless mishaps that are part and parcel of everyday emotional struggle.

Hurt, Anger, Shame, and Guilt

Unfortunately, love and sex aren't the only feelings we have to deal with. On the seamier side of our emotional life lie the so-called negative emotions—hurt, anger, shame, guilt—emotions that men have even more difficulty admitting to than sex and love. Such feelings as hurt, shame, and anger are commonplace to anyone whose love has been abused, whether man or woman. Men especially have these emotions when women rebuff their sexual advances, which, as we know, is often.

In the *Hite Report on Male Sexuality*, men answer the question "Would you like to change sex in any way? Has sex been everything you want it to be, or do you want it more?" I was very moved by the strong feelings that were expressed, certainly the strongest in the whole study. The men were plaintive, hurt, self-deprecating, and angry. . . .

"I guess I am a pig. . . . "

"I begged, pleaded, cajoled, but nothing worked. . . . "

"I don't cry anymore, because I don't care anymore."

"I fit the old American stereotype, 'oversexed and underfucked.'"

"Many women look upon sex as a chore to bring about the excretion of a little vile snivel with a kind of convulsion and considerable writhing."

"In some way I feel like I'm oversexed and some kind of maniac and I put myself down."

"I felt totally inadequate and useless. . . . "

"It is disgusting to resort to masturbation when you are sleeping with a woman every night. . . . "

". . . I feel she sometimes uses sex as a weapon. . . . "

"Sometimes . . . I come across as a woman hater, I feel chained to my sex drive. I feel cheated that someone can laughingly say no when I'm in my greatest need. . . . Sometimes, the only way to stop frustration is to say 'The hell with it.'"

Other revealing questions were "Do you usually make the initial sexual advance? How do you feel about it?

How do you feel if the other person does not want to have sex with you?" The answers again were full of hurt and anger and self-deprecation:

"I feel quite hurt, my self-esteem is lowered considerably."

"I get angry."

"I feel rejected."

"I *hate* making sexual advances. It makes me feel vulgar and crude."

"I usually feel like a jerk. . . . "

"If I'm rejected, I feel like a total fool. I feel like apologizing to the woman and slinking off to a corner like the lecherous scum she must think I am."

". . . I hate it!!!"

"I feel . . . embarrassed . . . angry . . . hurt. . . . "

Clearly, we have a serious, widespread problem here. Men want more sex and women want more feeling. But if men were to say how they feel, they would likely be furious, hurt, self-flagellating. This pervasive hurt and anger are, in my opinion, the emotional source of rape and other violence against women. When a man feels deprived whether by women or by life in general, he may decide in a misogynist rage to take revenge on a member of the "opposite sex."

Surely hurt and anger are not what women want to hear from men. The feelings they want are feelings of love, tenderness, affection. No wonder men and women throw their hands up in despair!

But wait, all is not lost. For if you read elsewhere, again in *The Hite Report on Male Sexuality*, you'll find that when asked, "Why do you like intercourse?" only three percent of the men mentioned orgasm at all. Nor did men often mention the pleasurable feeling of the vagina on the penis as the main reason. "Most of the men who

answered gave physical closeness and overall body contact—full-length embracing—as the most important
physical element of their liking intercourse," while "the
psychological/emotional reason most men gave for liking and wanting intercourse was the *feeling of being loved
and accepted* [italics mine] that intercourse gave them."

"I love the closeness that intercourse brings."

"To lie upon her and feel her body against mine with
the warmth of her and the feeling of her soft belly against
mine . . . I feel an ache for her just thinking about it."

"The being close to another is more important than
orgasm."

"I like intercourse for all its human contact."

"It makes me feel valuable."

"It makes me feel clean and whole, a part of life not
just a wanderer."

"The end of loneliness . . ."

"Knowing you are loved, knowing you can love."

"It's the point at which I feel she totally loves me."

"The feeling of someone liking you enough to give
their body to you."

"With my cock deep inside her I feel totally secure
and loved."

"Intercourse feels psychologically like acceptance to
me."

"It tells me she loves me. It gives confidence. . . . "

"It lets me express feelings of affection, warmth, tenderness and appreciation of women. . . ."

Hite concluded that "men look forward to sex and
intercourse as providing an appropriate time and place
to be emotional. The fact that this is almost men's only
time to be emotional and 'let their hair down' may account, in some measure, for men's feeling that they
rarely get enough sex and intercourse."

Due to our cultural upbringing, men yearn for the genital embrace because we find surcease, in a way we cannot achieve elsewhere, for our deep longing for love. Little wonder that we pursue it so relentlessly, and that when frustrated we feel such anger and humiliation.

Let no one who reads these words interpret them as an apology for men's often heartless sex-seeking behavior; it is merely a sympathetic viewing of our feelings. To repeat, when men obsessively chase after sex, it is because it's the only experience available through which our own feelings of intimacy and acceptance are given full vent.

When we become aware of the way in which our pursuit of sex affects women, we often respond with guilt. Guilt with respect to women is a major emotion in men and supposedly serves to curb our cheating, lying, and double-dealing hearts. It is allegedly a beneficial emotion often encouraged by women as their only leverage against men's lowly instincts. However, many women we interviewed disagree:

"Sure, if guilt is the only thing that will cause men to behave decently, let them feel guilty. But who wants to hang out with a guy who feels guilty about everything he wants?"

"Self-sufficient, powerful women don't want men to behave like good little boys just because they feel guilty about what they want. They would prefer that men acknowledge what they want, and ask for it openly instead of suppressing it with guilt."

"I can't stand it when men edge a little closer, and a little closer, and sneak up on you, all the time feeling guilty and pretending it's not happening. I'd just as soon they'd be overt, without being aggressive; that way I can make up my own mind."

108

When men feel guilty about their desires and suppress them, they may be acting acceptably, but they will also be devious and listless. It would be far better if a man said, "Listen Mary, I want to level with you. I am turned on to you and want to make love. I feel guilty about it, but it's true. Telling you is embarrassing and also scares me because I'm afraid you are going to turn me down."

Or he may feel guilty because he is *not* turned on to Mary or because he is turned on to Mary's friend Rebecca. He may feel guilty because he wants to play with his computer or go out with the boys instead of talking after dinner or because he masturbates or is smoking too much dope, drinking too much booze, or snorting too much coke.

Whatever the basis, when guilt is not expressed it will make him a dull boy, no fun to be around, closed up to emotional dialogue and difficult to comprehend. Guilt is also a poor motivator for change, and an even poorer substitute for it.

"I'm sick of him apologizing when he messes up. He feels real guilty; he is at the verge of tears sometimes, and of course I forgive him, fool that I am."

Another woman said, "I am so hungry for some feeling from him that I give in when he feels guilty. Then everything is supposedly all right, and before you know it, he does it again."

Contrition after wife beating, bingeing, irresponsibility, and other tresspasses is usually an uproductive emotion. At least when guilt is felt before the act and prevents it from happening, it has some value. But after the deed is done, guilt is a cheap and insufficient substitute for the changes that are needed.

In my opinion, we should be good men because it

109

will benefit us and the women and children (and men) we love. If for some reason we aren't good, it is far more useful to resolve not to repeat our reprehensible behavior, whatever it is, than to feel guilty. We must begin by acknowledging what we are. Once we do this, we can try to adjust to what women want us to be, provided they will meet us halfway with reasonable adjustments of their own. This can only be done through open, honest, principled, cooperative, and emotionally literate dialogue and negotiation. The old social contracts between the sexes can in that manner be updated and brought in line with the realities of modern men and women.

Sexuality, love, hurt, anger, shame, and guilt are some of the emotions that we feel and that women want us to be aware of, express, and deal with. They are right, because only by knowing what one's feelings are and how they do affect our behavior can we begin to acknowledge their influence on our relationships.

In fact, it can be argued that humankind's (rather than mankind's) progress depends on sensible reincorporation of the emotions into every situation of importance, including the family, the schools, and the higher levels of government. We have brought the world to the brink of nuclear holocaust through scientific and technical pursuits in which emotion was deemed irrelevant. It is time now to deal with the power and significance of the emotions. To know people's feelings is to be able to understand and predict their behavior more accurately. To know how to express one's own emotions effectively makes us effective in getting what we want. Emotional literacy is a major skill and a source of power for human beings.

In the arena of men-women relations, when women

say that they want feelings from men, they are referring concretely to men's capacity to love and to say they do and to their capacity to accept a woman's love and respond to it appropriately. Of course, it isn't just loving feelings that interest women, but it is love that is at the center of the emotions women want from men.

And the point, of course, is not just to mouth the words as many men have learned to do, but to develop an ease with one's emotions that makes it possible to feel love and to say "I love you" without fear of ridicule or rejection. This includes the capacity to love someone who may not love you; the capacity to clarify, when one loves someone, just how much—whether just now or forever—the capacity to say "I love you" without feeling automatically committed to a lifetime relationship, and the capacity, finally, to say "I don't love you" when that is the case.

Being able to say "I love you" will free you to say "I hate you." There may be hurt, humiliation, and shame when we are not loved in return. We may feel guilt when a person we loved yesterday is no longer loved by us today, or joy and exuberance when a person we love, loves us back. Having once expressed our loving feelings, the whole network of allied emotions will become a part of our lives; all of those feelings in turn will need to be expressed and dealt with.

Learning emotional literacy is not an overnight matter; it takes time and has many lessons to be explored. But the main lesson is learning to say "I love you" when love is felt and to deal with inhibitions, fears, and second thoughts truthfully and responsibly.

CHAPTER 11

EMOTIONAL

LITERACY

The term *literacy* is ordinarily applied to the capacity to read and write. But it can also be applied to the knowledge of other matters including emotions. Emotional literacy, the capacity to understand and deal with emotions, is a skill that women value highly when it is present in men.

An emotionally illiterate man will not know his own emotions and what causes them. He will have no control over the extent to which his emotions express themselves. He will not be aware of other people's feelings and what causes them. And when other people express themselves emotionally, he will not know what to do. An emotionally illiterate person will not be able to communicate his emotions and will not know what to do when he is overwhelmed by them.

Consider Lucas, a 38-year-old accountant who consulted me with his wife for a mediation of their marital difficulties. His wife, Clara, had just given a tight-lipped, tearful account of her anger and hurt about the way things were between them. I turned to him. He looked stiff and uncomfortable.

"How do you feel, Lucas?"

"Well, I feel that she is being unfair."

"Okay. We'll talk about that later, when we get your point of view, but how does the way she talks make you feel?"

He hesitates, wriggles in his chair, thinks. Finally, looking embarrassed, he adds: "I guess I don't feel anything."

"I doubt it. Let's see, do you have any sensations in your body? Some people feel lumps in their stomach, funny sensations..."

"Well, I feel sort of numb all over. Not now so much but when she was talking."

"Good, what else?"

"And I also feel a tight band around my forehead."

"Okay. Do you think that it makes you angry when she talks like that?"

"Yeah, angry, I suppose."

"How about hurt?"

"I guess so. . . . Yeah, hurt and angry," he says with emphasis.

Lucas is a fairly typical example of garden-variety emotional illiteracy. He eventually learned a great deal about his emotions and Clara's.

At the other extreme of the literacy scale, an emotionally aware man will be conscious of experiencing a variety of emotions at a variety of intensities. He will know what he feels and why. For instance, when he is afraid, he will know when he is mildly anxious or when he is terrified, and he will know why. He will also know how to make these feelings clear to others, as well as *how* and *when* to express them most productively. If another person is not expressing emotions freely, he will know how to investigate what they are. He will know the effect of the combinations of his and another person's emotions, and be able to avoid those situations in which feelings escalate catastrophically. On the other hand, he will also know how emotions can combine between people in a harmonious and positive manner.

A person who cannot read often becomes afraid and defensive about his incapacity and fakes understanding out of embarrassment. Illiterate persons tend to invalidate the importance of reading and writing and often become anti-literate and discount the value of the written word. People who are illiterate often try to compensate in other ways; they try to live a normal life outside of the realm of letters. However, they are never able to escape the fact that they are unable to understand or communicate through the written word.

Likewise, emotionally illiterate persons are often embarrassed by their incapacity and attempt to compensate for their handicap through logical and rational methods. They discount emotions as being meaningless and useless and are embarrassed and defensive when their incapacity is revealed. Since emotional illiteracy is the rule rather than the exception, the anti-emotional consensus acts as a powerful reinforcement of the illiterate condition.

After some months of work, Lucas, reflecting on his emotional upbringing, said: "I remember as a boy being proud of acting like my father and not like my mother. I even imitated how he sat when my mother hassled him with tears and scenes. Later, in the service, I was proud of being very calm, not ice-cold like some guys but calm. We all had contempt for guys who got excited or upset. I notice, lately, that soldier movies make a big thing out of the sergeant having feelings. Ours didn't, I'll tell you that for sure."

The consequences of emotional illiteracy are many. On one hand, when emotions are not acknowledged but suppressed instead, human relationships become one-dimensional, cold, simplified.

Rationality and logic prevail at the overt public level. Interactions seem "civilized" and "grown up." But barely hidden beneath the surface, emotions do continue to exist and create the effects of their presence. When suppressed, pent-up emotions distort thinking and communication, produce erratic behavior, and even create physical symptoms such as head-, back-, and stomach-aches and chronic conditions like arthritis, ulcers, colitis, and hypertension. Heart disease and some forms of cancer may also be the result of inadequately expressed feelings, as can depression and addiction to drugs.

As emotionally illiterate human beings, many men discount and deny their emotions. When we lose track of what we really want in order to go along with other people's wishes, we eventually become angry and persecute them. When events hurt or sadden us and we cannot cry, that sadness becomes the bedrock of our personality. We become walking dead, forever depressed and joyless. When our impulse to embrace, love and kiss, and celebrate our loved ones is denied, our hearts shrink. We become attached to inanimate objects that we can then love, discard, and replace with minimal pain.

Our lives may appear to be orderly, productive, and well organized, but our emotions are in shambles. Our homes, bedrooms, and kitchens are neat and clean, but our closets are piled high with psychic junk and our basements are cluttered with emotional dung. We understand the trajectory of rockets and bombs. We can compute megadeaths. But we cannot direct our loving energies at home, at the office, or across the negotiating table. We have the most advanced medical system in the world, but we have forgotten how to die with dignity.

Alienated from their emotional nature, people become living dead—alive physically but morally deceased. Emotions are unavailable to the emotionally illiterate, but power isn't. Being unaware and unconcerned with feelings gives people a heartless advantage over others who are restrained by their scruples. And when the living dead acquire power, as they so often do, they subject the rest of us to their control, power plays, and violence. When the emotionally illiterate inhabit the corridors of power and dominate whole governments, they threaten the citizenry with apocalypse—war, death, hunger, and disease.

Evaluating Your Emotional Literacy

More concretely, I may love a woman and she may love me. We may be fantastic lovers and make fabulous love, but unless we understand and effectively deal with our emotions, our relationship will deteriorate. It'll either unravel relentlessly until there's nothing but loose ends, or it'll become a trap from which only divorce or death can release us.

You may wonder where you stand on the emotional literacy scale. Here is a questionnaire that may help you find out:

1. Do your feelings sometimes get out of control? Anger? Tears? Depression? Do your feelings puzzle you? Are you unable to understand them?

116

2. Do you sometimes feel empty inside, or dead—that you are missing something very important in life?

3. Do people complain that you lack feeling, that you are cold? Arrogant? Rejecting?

4. Do you find that most of your relationships with women are like turns at the bat—"Three strikes and you're out!"? Do you have trouble getting involved with a woman beyond a few dates?

5. Do you experience your feelings of love coming and going inexplicably and uncontrollably?

6. Are you embarrassed asking for what you want or talking about being hurt? Do you have trouble saying, "I love you"?

7. Do you avoid emotional situations like goodbyes or people who are grieving or sick? Do you have trouble crying? Are you embarrassed when someone shows affection for you in public?

If you answered yes to these questions, you have some of the most common symptoms of emotional illiteracy. The more of these experiences you are familiar with, the more you will be able to profit from this section of the book.

What We Feel and Why

To be emotionally literate we need not only to feel, but to know. We need to know both what it is that we are feeling and what the causes for our feelings are. It is not sufficient to know that we are angry, guilty, happy, or in love. We also need to know the origin of our anger, what causes our guilt, why we are in love.

Let's begin by learning to determine *what* we are feeling. There is no convincing final word on precisely how many different emotions there are; an exact taxonomy remains to be developed. But it is fairly clear that there

117

are at most three handfuls of primary emotions—that is to say, emotions that are reasonably distinct from each other—including love, anger, fear, joy, shame, guilt, pride, sadness, hurt, confidence, and hatred.

To begin with, emotions can be divided into positive and negative, depending on whether we seek them or avoid them because they give us pleasure or pain. Every positive emotion seems to have a negative counterpart. For example, love is the positive counterpart of hatred. Shame is a negative emotion; pride is the positive counterpart. Likewise, guilt and self-righteousness, hurt and well-being, sadness and happiness, fear and confidence—all line up on the positive and negative sides of the same spectrum. When two or more primary emotions occur simultaneously, they combine into secondary emotional hues. Love can occur with shame or with anger or even with its counterpart, hate. When more emotions are added, they can create such a muddy experience that chaos and confusion are the consequence. Jealousy is often such a compost of emotions—anger, fear, shame, love, sexual desire—that it is both incomprehensible and unmanageable.

Emotions can also be strong or weak. Each of the emotions mentioned above has powerful and weak manifestations. For instance, anger can go from minor irritation to blind rage. Shame can go from slight embarrassment to intense blush-provoking humiliation. People who are emotionally illiterate may recognize their emotions only at the very intense end of the spectrum.

Men, for instance, are often either completely unaware of mild forms of anger or unable to speak about them. Yet, when they get angry enough, men will express their anger and know that they are feeling it. The same is true of men's awareness of and capacity to express their feelings of love. Men have a tendency to feel love only when it is at the very intense end of the spectrum, and to feel it very intensely but, when the feeling wanes, suddenly find themselves utterly out of love.

As in a CB radio, where all signals of a certain intensity or less are completely suppressed and only those that are strong enough will break through and be heard, people with a high level of emotional squelch will experience themselves as having no major feelings for the most part of their waking lives. With the exception of sudden breakthroughs at certain dramatic moments, they experience their lives as rational and emotionally free. They tend to see occasional experiences of irrepressible emotion as unpredictable, highly unwanted disruptions in their everyday lives, and are not aware of the constant interplay of emotions below the level of consciousness that is the cause for the outbursts.

Figure 1 is a graphic example of what I am trying to explain. In a typical day, Lucas may have many emotions taking place in his body, but he is aware of only the tips of his emotional iceberg. One brief experience of love in the morning; another of anger in the afternoon.

Another example, a man who is in love with a woman who is being less than candid about her affections for another man may after weeks or months suddenly explode into a jealous rage. The blinding feeling that overcomes him is a combination of strong emotions: of love and anger because of her unfair treatment, of envy and jealousy because he feels that she is giving her love to another, of humiliation because of his powerlessness, and of rage because of her deceit. All of these together will be experienced as an amorphous and overwhelming emotional chaos that he'll likely want to suppress because of its unmanageable nature.

If he had been more emotionally literate, he might have noticed his feelings several weeks before and expressed, rather than hidden, them. He would have known the specific feelings involved and their intensity and how they combined with each other. That is:

1. he is very much in love,

2. he feels needy of her attention,

3. he is suspicious of his beloved's relationship with another, and

4. these three feelings—love, neediness, and suspicion—led to fear, hurt, and anger and combined into jealousy.

Knowing this, he might have been able to express these feelings earlier when they were at a much lower level of intensity. If he had, she might have changed the course of her actions: She might have been more aware that he really loves her. She might have decided to treat him more honestly and clarified her feelings about him. One way or another his expressions of feeling could have made the uncontrollable breakthrough less likely and could also have alerted her to his feelings so that she could do something about them. But how was he to determine these emotional facts when he didn't really know about his feelings in the first place?

Learning Emotional Literacy

There is a strong tendency in our culture to denigrate the learning of emotional skills, especially for men. A man who wants to learn about these matters is not going to receive a lot of support in his everyday life.

Learning emotional literacy in our unsympathetic environment will be difficult. Expressions or inquiries about emotions will be deflected or discounted, and there won't be many interested in assisting with the task. It's important to remember that in order to learn emotional literacy it is helpful to be in an emotionally nurturing environment in which people applaud and support the learning of these skills. Therefore, a major first step is to find such an environment.

Friends, church groups, men's groups, a human potential workshop, or a supportive therapy group can be the source of backup for men who want to learn emotional literacy. A nurturing lover can be very helpful, of course, but should not be the only support, since emotional learning can be exhausting for the teacher. It's a good idea to take the pressure off the single lover, who can then be helpful without being central to the process. There are also situations in which whole families and groups of people are open to emotional dialogue; such cooperative environments are ideal for learning emotional literacy.

Like any complex skill, it takes time and patience to learn emotional literacy. Ideally, it would be learned during childhood in an emotionally literate environment. When it's not, as is generally the case, several complications emerge. First, when learning does not occur at the developmentally appropriate age, it will be more difficult later. Second, while failing to develop the skill, the child will probably develop poor habits that will need to be *unlearned* before learning can occur. When people learn to play an instrument or type or read on their own, they often have to go through a difficult period of unlearning counter-productive habits before further effective learning can occur.

This is also true of emotional literacy; it is more difficult to learn later in life and requires unlearning certain bad emotional habits that interfere with it. However, while difficult, the task is far from impossible given the desire and resolve to do so.

Unlearning Emotional Power Abuse

Emotions have power. They have an impact that at times can be overwhelming to others. We are aware of the power of emotions when we hold them back so as not to upset their target. We abuse power when we unload them without warning on the unwary, unprepared, or unprotected.

We further abuse our emotions' power when we use them in power plays that are a sort of emotional blackmail, a tactic used to intimidate others into some form of compliance. To give our feelings more power and justification, we couple them with judgments, accusations, exaggerations, and lies, and we wield them like clubs.

For instance, when John is slow in doing the evening's dishes, Mary would do best to say something like: "John, we agreed that if I cooked, you would do the dishes, and you are making me angry the way you are dragging the job out; please do as we agreed and finish the dishes."

But because she is feeling frustrated and powerless, and in order to get him to do as they agreed, she might say: "Goddammit, John, I am getting sick and tired of your dragging your feet. I can't believe how far you'll go not to do your share around here; you are setting a fine example of laziness for the kids, is all I can say. . . . "

Common sense indicates that other people affect us emotionally. Yet, it has been said that it is not possible for one person to make another person feel something. Some pop psychologists argue that only you can make yourself happy, for instance, or that if someone gets you angry, it's only because you allow it. According to this theory, John and Mary are ultimately and completely responsible for how they feel.

When you think about this, however, it seems obvious that one person's actions can create emotions in another. If Mary suddenly starts yelling about the dishes in the middle of a pleasant conversation with John, he is very likely to react emotionally. Perhaps after being scared, he will feel hurt, and after feeling hurt, he will be angry. Meanwhile John's feelings are affecting Mary, who might respond with guilt, anger, or hopelessness. All these reactions will be the consequence of Mary's outburst. Emotions have real energy that sets up a powerful field of influence and affects people in its physical vicinity.

John, for example, has practically no choice but to feel scared when Mary suddenly shouts at him about the dishes. The hurt and later anger may be optional, but all three feelings are the consequence, to some extent, of her behavior.

A common response of an emotionally illiterate person to another person's feelings is to disclaim responsibility. If John is scared, hurt, or angry, Mary's reaction may be "That is your problem," or "You are choosing to be angry," because she feels no duty to respond or react to them. This discounts the whole realm of emotional responsibility and flies in the face of the obvious interconnections between people. Women often complain of such responses coming from men and feel them to be major obstacles to emotional dialogue.

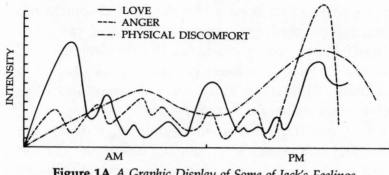

Figure 1A *A Graphic Display of Some of Jack's Feelings in the Course of a Day*

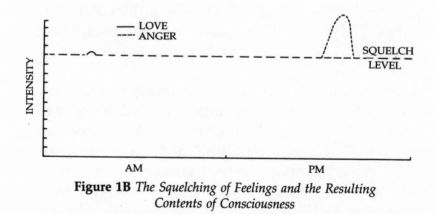

Figure 1B *The Squelching of Feelings and the Resulting Contents of Consciousness*

The truth is that we are able to cause feelings in other people, and they can cause feelings in us. That capacity can be abused when we assault each other with anger, or try to create guilt with our hurt. Only when this is acknowledged can an emotionally literate dialogue occur. To deny this fact is a form of emotional illiteracy.

People are intimately affected by each other's emotions, whether or not these emotions are fully acknowledged. In fact, it is probably true that the less the emotions are discussed, the more they are discounted and the more they affect their hosts.

The discounting of emotions can take several forms. On one hand we can discount our own. We may know that we are feeling something, but we purposely brush it aside. Doing this can lead to the gradual loss of awareness that we are feeling at all. On the other hand, we can discount other people's feelings. Here again we may be aware that another person is having a strong emotion and decide to ignore it, or we may have lost the capacity of being aware of other people's feelings altogether.

Even when discounted, however, the emotions continue. People think they interact rationally, but at the same time, at a very real but unacknowledged level, the emotional dialogue proceeds on another channel with its own puzzling consequences. One major consequence of discounting emotions is that they can stimulate each other and snowball and eventually rage out of control. Some people feel that emotional outbursts of this sort are a healthy blowout that cleans the system of emotional trash. In a way, it is true that such outbursts release some of the tension of discounted feelings, but usually somebody gets hurt in the process, often women or children, leaving behind emotional wounds and scars that sometimes never heal.

It takes emotional literacy to understand and direct the emotional dialogue, the feeling content of a relationship. Consider the following statement.

"You have been *absolutely impossible* today. I'm ready to *throw in the towel*."

This sentence, said in anger, contains an exaggeration ("absolutely"), a judgment ("impossible"), and a metaphor ("throw in the towel"). Clearly, the person is angry and probably has reason enough, but the power plays with which the anger is expressed are an example of emotional illiteracy.

The above statement is unlikely to communicate what the person is really feeling, how intensely, or why. It is even less likely to bring about a solution to the problem that evidently exists between the two people. It is more likely to invite a response in kind. For example:

"Oh, yeah? Well have you looked at yourself in the mirror lately? You have been such a bitch that you're lucky I'm still around. Go ahead, leave, see if I care, but do it soon because I may be gone by the time you do..." etc.

Again, this response contains no clear message of what the person is feeling, how strongly, or why. Instead, it is an escalation of chaotic emotions (hurt and anger), self-righteousness, power plays, blaming, insults, name-calling, exaggeration, threats, and judgments. Much better would be to say: "Now wait a minute. I want to say something. When you talk like that, when you say that I have been absolutely impossible and talk about throwing in the towel, that makes me really angry, you hurt my feelings, and you scare me. What is your point? What is bothering you?"

This last statement may seem clumsy but it is an emotionally literate response that will produce positive

126

problem-solving responses. It avoids three major errors by doing the following.

1. It *warns* the recipient that something is about to be said, and therefore, it is more likely to fall on sympathetic ears. ("Now wait a minute. I want to say something.")

2. It *describes* the *emotions* being experienced without judgments, accusations, exaggerations, or power plays. (Angry, hurt, scared.)

3. It *describes* the *actions* that are the cause of the emotions being felt, thus leaving little doubt about the reasons for the feelings. ("When you talk like that, when you say that I have been absolutely impossible and talk about throwing in the towel.")

By doing all of the above without judgments, or power abuse, this way of talking creates an optimal climate for emotionally literate, problem-solving dialogue.

Dealing with Everyday Emotional Transactions

To deal with some of the major emotional issues ordinarily not attended to in people's everyday social transactions, it is necessary to know:

1. What and how strongly we feel.

2. What other people are doing to contribute to how we feel.

3. Our intuitive suspicions and explanations about what causes other people's actions.

4. What it is that we want and don't want from people.

5. How to listen to and assimilate all of the above when we are the recipient.

For instance, after a hard day's work, Anthony comes home and finds that Sandy, instead of being home as he hoped, is working late with a new account. Anthony is disappointed, hurt, frustrated. He wants to strangle

Sandy, her boss, and the new account. Realizing that he is irrationally angry, he suppresses his fury. He suspects that the boss is keeping Sandy at the office because he is turned on to her and that she reciprocates his attraction. He assumes that the two of them and the new account are having a rip-roaring dinner party at his favorite restaurant.

When she finally comes home, he is calm but sullen and lifeless. He responds with irritation to her enthusiasm about the new account and does not acknowledge her apology for leaving him stranded.

The essentials of an emotional literate dialogue require that he:

1. Tell her how he felt when he got home—hurt, angry, humiliated.

2. What she did that caused his feelings—stay out late with the boss on short notice.

3. What he suspects is going on with the boss—carrying on a flirtation.

4. What he wants her to do next time—call him at work and give him some warning.

If, in turn, she responds in an emotionally literate way, she will:

5. Listen sympathetically without defensiveness, acknowledge how he feels, and validate whatever truth there may be in his suspicions.

If all these steps are taken, the likelihood is that this difficult situation will be dealt with in a positive way, and that Anthony and Sandy will be able to continue their relationship in harmony. If not, and emotional chaos is allowed to take place, this incident could be the beginning of the disintegration of their relationship.

And now for the basics of emotional literacy.

| SEVEN BASIC

STEPS TO

EMOTIONAL

LITERACY

Here are some simple exercises that break down the process of learning emotional literacy, step by step. They are like training wheels on a child's bicycle that make the complicated task easier to master.

The seven basic steps are:

1. Asking for permission to deliver an emotionally laden statement.

2. Making a statement without judgment or accusation in which we inform another person of how we felt in connection with what he or she did.

3. Accepting without defensiveness another person's statement about how our actions felt.

4. Telling another person of an intuition, theory, or suspicion about what he is doing or why he is doing it.

5. Validating another person's intuition, theory, or suspicion by searching for its truth rather than denying it.

6. Apologizing for committing an error.

7. Accepting an apology.

1. Asking for Permission. Whenever you are planning to say anything relating to your emotions, whether positive or negative, always prepare the person, preferably by specifying what you are about to say.

Example: "Can I tell you something I like about you?" or "I have been feeling something that upsets me lately. Can I tell you?" or "There is something going on between us that I don't like. Are you interested in hearing about it?"

When asking a person's permission to speak in this manner, we are a) giving him a warning that something difficult is coming, b) giving him a choice as to whether he wants to deal with it at this time, and c) giving him a chance to prepare himself and be ready to listen. When we follow this approach, we are ensuring that our statements will fall on fertile soil and will have a chance to generate productive responses. There has to be a genuine choice. We need to be willing to accept that the timing of our statement might not be particularly good and to wait for a better moment. Also, we are avoiding, as far as is possible, guilt, defensiveness, and anger in the other person.

2. Making an Action/Feeling Statement. An action/feeling statement describes in one simple, understandable sentence what emotion occurred in connection with another person's action. "When you [*action*], I felt [*emotion*]." This statement is designed to inform the person of an emotion or emotions you had in association with his or her behavior. It is designed not to provoke guilt or defensiveness because it contains no judgment, accusation, or reproach.

An action/feeling statement simply states that a ver-

130

ifiable action resulted in an undeniable feeling. For instance:

John: "When you wanted to stop talking on the phone last night, I felt hurt at first, and then angry."

Assuming that Mary can agree she hung up the phone yesterday, and that she understands how John felt (hurt and angry), this statement will have been successful in its purpose: to provide Mary with information about how John felt last night when she hung up. It is a way for John to be heard, and to express his feelings in a way that doesn't hurt or abuse Mary.

In the expression of an action/feeling statement, a number of errors can be made.

Error A. Confusing Action and Motivation. When attempting to describe an action, it is possible to go beyond a simple statement, such as, "When you hung up the telephone," or "When you arrived late," or "When you interrupted me," and add to it a judgment, such as: "When you so *rudely* hung up on me," or "When you *humiliated* me by being late," or "When you *showed your disregard for my opinion* by interrupting me." One thus includes information of a completely different nature than the description of an action. These judgments constitute a theory about the other person's motivation and a judgment about those reasons. These elaborations are likely to get you into trouble because they may be incorrect and because they judge and blame and will create guilt, anger, and other complications that it is the purpose of this exercise to avoid. Step No. 4, outlined below, is designed to express these intuitions, fears about other people's motivation, and paranoid fantasies. But these should not be included with the action/feeling statement so as not to cloud the emotional landscape.

Error B. Confusion of Feeling and Thought. In trying to express a feeling, we often name a thought instead.

For instance: "When you interrupted our conversation, *I felt that you were angry*," or "When you interrupted our conversation, *I felt that you weren't interested in what I had to say*."

These aren't feelings at all; they're again thoughts, theories about what was going on with the other person at the time. A proper feeling would be anger, fear, or shame, in varying degrees.

A more subtle version of this confusion is a statement such as: "When you interrupted our conversation, *I felt rejected*," which is an error as well.

"Feeling rejected" is not really a statement of a feeling and does not give an idea of what you were feeling. Were you angry? Were you sad? Were you embarrassed? Were you ashamed? When you say that you *felt* rejected, you are saying that the other person rejected you, and you are stating a theory about the other person's motivation; a desire to reject you. This is a thought rather than an emotion. No one can argue with you if you say that you experienced a certain feeling, assuming that you are being truthful. But a theory about why the other person is doing something may be incorrect.

3. Accepting an Action/Feeling Statement. For an emotionally literate communication to be effective, it has to be received as well as sent. You might ask yourself why Mary should care about John's feeling. You might tell yourself that this kind of disclosure is self-indulgent and immature. But that would be discounting John's feelings, and we already know the kind of trouble ignoring people's feelings can cause. An emotionally literate recipient of such an expression will take careful

132

note of the emotion and when it happened. Mary may already know that John was angry and hurt, or she might be surprised. She may understand why he feels this way, or she may be puzzled by it. In any case, all she needs is to have the information and to acknowledge it. Then she can start the process of emotional dialogue in which feelings are given proper recognition. By doing this, Mary learns about John's responses to situations, and she gives him an opportunity to let go of his bad feeling.

In the above case of Mary and John, it will suffice for Mary to acknowledge that, yes, she understands that when she wanted to stop talking, John felt hurt and angry. This acknowledgment can be in the form of a nod or by saying, "I hear you," or "I understand that when I ended the conversation, you felt hurt, and then angry."

But let's say John says, "When you so rudely hung up yesterday, I felt that you didn't care even a little bit for me."

In order to extract an action/feeling statement from the above, Mary will have to ignore the judgments and accusation.

She might respond, "Now wait, let me get this straight. You are saying that when I stopped our conversation yesterday, which I remember doing, you felt something, but I don't know what. Were you angry?"

"No, I felt you were being rude."

"Okay, your opinion is that I was being rude, but would you be willing to tell me how you felt? I'm interested in how you felt at the time."

"I don't know. I felt that you didn't like me."

"Well, you still haven't told me how you felt."

"Hurt, and then angry."

"Okay, now I know what I wanted to know; you felt hurt and angry."

By now, you, dear reader, may say: "People don't talk like that in the real world, maybe in California, but not anywhere I know. I'm not willing to talk like that. I'd be embarrassed to death."

That's a fine action/feeling statement: "When speaking in an emotionally literate way, I feel embarrassment." I recognize the problem and can only agree with you: People don't usually talk that way and it is embarrassing and difficult at times. What can I say beyond *that it works?*

What does it do? It creates a favorable climate for emotional expression coupled with rationality. It cools down unruly emotions, gives people an opportunity to express these emotions in a way least likely to result in further hurt, and lays the groundwork for further safe, productive, emotional dialogue. It informs people of each other's emotional topography—the lay of the land in the world of their feelings—so that they can more easily find their way around in it in the future.

Error C. Defensiveness and Guilt. The ever-present danger in being the recipient of another's feeling/action statements, especially if imperfectly formulated, is guilt and defensiveness.

"I thought you were done talking; that's why I wanted to stop," or "Rude? What's so rude about ending a conversation? You were being rude by talking on and on about your troubles with Anne," or "Angry? You have a lot of nerve being angry. I should be angry about the waste of my time," or "Hurt? Don't be so self-indulgent," and so on.

These responses are beside the point. First things first.

134

If Mary feels misunderstood, guilty, or angry, she can talk about that later. Right now what matters are John's feelings, not Mary's. It is just a matter of taking turns. First, it is important that Mary acknowledge what John felt when she wanted to stop talking. Then, she can talk about how she felt.

Sometimes not being defensive is very difficult. It requires biting one's tongue and talking oneself into patience and forbearance. But it is worth doing for the sake of a continuing orderly dialogue. It cools down the potential escalation of emotionally laden conversations and gives empathy an opportunity to come to the surface. But more importantly, it is the only fair thing to do when a friend or loved one is in emotional distress.

4. **Expressing your Intuitions.** The above conversational suggestions are designed to express action/feeling statements to the exclusion of all other potentially confusing material. But surely, we can't speak very long without dealing with our suspicions about other people's motivations and intentions. The next step in emotionally literate dialogue is designed to deal with them.

In our daily lives we are constantly trying to make sense of other people's behavior. When we are not in good communication with them, we are forced to make up theories and guess what they are up to by using our intuition and whatever information is available. We don't normally go to the people in question and investigate why they are doing whatever they are doing. We don't because we don't know how and don't trust that we'll get an honest answer if we do.

Behind John's hurt and anger about Mary's ending their phone conversation, there is a fear, perhaps an assumption, that Mary doesn't like him. Having once stated how he felt and when, he could now (after asking

135

for permission) express these fears as follows:

"I have a fear that you don't like me, that you are angry at me."

This states what I call a paranoid fantasy. It puts in an objective manner an intuition about what the other person is thinking or feeling. It is stated tentatively, not as a fact, but as an intuition that may in fact be mistaken or ill conceived. The intuition may be incorrect, but it is real because it exists in the speaker's mind. Its reality has to be acknowledged, and its truth should be evaluated. Since people's intuitions are rarely completely mistaken, it gives the recipient the opportunity to search his or her own consciousness to see if there is some truth in it.

Paranoia is considered a form of madness. When it presents itself in the full-blown form of a persistent delusion of persecution (for example, The F.B.I., C.I.A., and K.G.B. are trying to poison me because of my political ideas), it is clearly associated with insanity.

In my opinion, paranoia has its origin in heightened awareness. Our intuition is a powerful reality-sensing tool. We are aware of many things that are never spoken of, or are discounted and denied by others. When we sense something and it is denied, we have two options. Either we forget whatever it is our intuition brought to our attention, or if we are stubborn and don't give up so easily, we persist in our idea. Perhaps we try to find our own answers. If we continue to get denials and dismissals of our intuitions, our efforts to figure out what's going on may lead us far off the mark, especially if we have an active imagination. As an example, John's simple intuition becomes elaborated from:

"Mary is unhappy," to

"Mary is unhappy with me," to

"Mary is angry with me," to

"Mary hates me."

Now John needs a reason for which Mary hates him. He talks to Nancy, Mary's best friend, who offhandedly guesses that Mary is bothered by John's sexy manner. That's it! John concludes: "Mary hates me because she thinks I'm a chauvinist pig."

Meanwhile, Mary hasn't got a clue about what is going on. In fact, she was short with John, but it had to do with being tired, and anxious about another phone call she was expecting, and slightly annoyed with John because he kept talking about his troubles with Ann.

So John's intuition was somewhat correct (as intuitions almost always are). Consequently, when he checks it out with Mary, she will be able to validate his experience to a certain extent. But suppose she does the usual in these circumstances. Suppose when he asks if she's angry, she answers, "Angry? Not at all. I feel fine. I like you, John."

Error D. Discounting an Intuition. This response, well-meaning as it may be, leaves John confused. Mary likes him (maybe), but what about his sense that there is something wrong? He'll have to forget about it.

Emotionally, this is a catastrophic event. Is he happy because Mary likes him (or so she says), or is he angry because she is denying that something is wrong? Does he trust her? Does he like her? It's enough to make his head spin. His mind is messed up and his emotions confused.

Confusion and heightened paranoia are the usual result of such a discount. On the other hand the discovery and acknowledgment of a grain of truth in the intuition has a clarifying effect.

5. Responding to an Intuition. Mary's correct, emotionally literate response would be to search for the grain of truth in John's intuition. What I mean by grain of truth is that part of the intuition that is correct, as opposed to the part that is off the mark. Hearing the grain of truth in his intuition will provide an explanation that will help John let go of the part that is truly paranoid. It will help him reconcile with reality by validating the portion of his experience that is valid.

In any event, Mary's above response to John's intuition does not validate his experience. He insists: "Somehow I thought something was amiss. Am I wrong?"

After thinking about it, Mary suggests: "Actually, John, I was angry after you called, not at you, but at Nancy—maybe that's it."

John may still not feel that this explains what he's thinking about the conversation. He goes on: "Well, that doesn't deal with my intuition that you were angry with me when we talked, *before* you spoke with Nancy. Was there something wrong while we were talking?"

This causes Mary to reconsider. Her annoyance with John was minor, but he does have a habit of going on and on over the phone. Since he seems willing to hear her criticism, maybe she can tell him without a lot of complications.

"Actually, no, I am not really angry at you. But when you called, I was tired and expecting another call, and slightly irritated with what you wanted to talk about. I thought I was giving you hints that I didn't want to talk about Ann, but you didn't seem to catch on. Does that make sense?"

John's reaction to this is one of relief. He was right; something was wrong. Mary is not angry at him, however, and he now knows what the problem was. He understands his and her feelings at the time and where they came from. He realizes he has tried her patience going on and on about Ann. He can now believe that she truly likes him. The facts of the situation and his feelings fit together like a jigsaw puzzle. He feels okay; he has been validated.

Sometimes the entire intuition will be correct.

"Yes, John, I am angry with you; in fact, I haven't liked you very much since I met you."

Harsh words indeed, but better for John to hear them clearly expressed than to have to live in a confusing and potentially hurtful climate.

They may go on to a discussion about why she doesn't like him, or about their relationship; his tendency to talk on and on and her inability to be clear when she doesn't want to talk. Or they may drop the matter. Either way, they are several steps ahead in the process of understanding each other, and have avoided the potential proliferation of paranoia and suspicion.

To recapitulate, in an emotionally literate dialogue, a person who has an intuition of something amiss, after asking permission, states it as an unconfirmed intuition seeking to be validated. The emotionally literate response to such an intuition is a search for and production of a validating grain of truth.

Whether John gets complete validation or not, he will feel better than when he started, if only because he tried. Future interactions with Mary may or may not improve matters. Most likely, if carried on in this emotionally literate way, they will. At any rate, the correct response to an intuition is an earnest and truthful search and statement of whatever may be going on in the recipient's emotional life that could possibly account for the intu-

139

ition expressed. It will help John let go of those parts that aren't true and will replace confusion with knowledge and information.

Being able to discuss each other's feelings can bring spectacular results when trouble develops between two people. When both people are committed to frank cooperative communication without power plays or lies, most emotionally difficult situations can be dealt with quickly and effectively.

6. Making an Apology. The next step concerns the fine art of acknowledging one's mistakes and begging for forgiveness for whatever harm we may have caused.

The thought of making a heartfelt apology strikes terror in the average man. Losing face, backing off, eating crow—all bring back memories of schoolyard struggles that tested and prepared us for our manhood. We have learned that standing one's ground is manly, that backing down is weak and humiliating. Yet, a truly emotionally literate man will admit his mistakes and apologize if he caused any harm. Being emotionally literate definitely goes against the old-fashioned stereotype of "being a man." Whenever you behave in an emotionally literate way you are choosing to change yourself into a different kind of a man, a man who acknowledges and deals with his emotions.

To go back to John and Mary's phone conversation, emotionally illiterate behavior does not occur in isolated transactions but in patterns. Two ways we engage in these patterns are to either a) do something we don't want to do, or b) do more than our share in a given situation. We rescue. We do these things for people whom we see as being victims unable to take responsibility for themselves. Sometimes we even rescue people who don't expect or want to be rescued.

In the situation between Mary and John, Mary could have rescued John by continuing the original phone conversation for another fifteen minutes, which, in addition to being something she did not want to do, might have caused her to miss Nancy's call. If she did rescue John, it would be because she assumed that he would be hurt or upset if she cut him short. She may have rescued John without John knowing it or particularly wanting to be rescued. The fact that he didn't like to be cut short does not imply that he would want her to continue a conversation she was not interested in.

The inevitable outcome of rescuing people is anger. Anger in the rescuer who gets fed up with doing things she doesn't want to do or with doing more than her share. And anger in the victim for being condescended to as someone who can't take care of himself. Inevitably, the rescuer will eventually persecute the victim, or the victim will persecute the rescuer. Anger will spill freely in all directions.

The best way of interrupting this cycle is to stop rescuing and apologize. But stopping rescuing is difficult. One has to know what one wants and doesn't want to do and what is a fair distribution of a relationship's responsibilities.

"Do I want to continue this conversation?"

"Do I want to have sex?"

"Do I want to help John fix the car?"

"Do I want to go to the ball game?"

"Do I want to eat out tonight?"

"Is it fair for me to do the dishes if Mary cooks, or should I also sweep the floor?"

"Is it fair that I always have to initiate sex?"

"Do I always pay for dinner when we go out? Do I want to?"

The correct thing to do when we discover that we have been rescuing is one of self-criticism rather than anger, an apology rather than an accusation. In addition, when we have rescued and want to stop, it is important to do so with a gentle, nurturing explanation rather than an abrupt withdrawal or sulk.

There are many times when we discover that we have made a mistake. At those times, the emotionally literate transaction is to acknowledge one's error and apologize by saying something, such as the following:

"When I [*action*] I made a mistake. I apologize."

Mary: "When I talked to you on the phone last night, after a few minutes I really didn't want to go on talking, so I started getting angry with you, even though it was my responsibility to let you know that I wanted to stop. I am sorry I let it go. I should have let you know earlier."

Error E. Blaming the Victim. Mary could have said: "Listen, John. I'm sorry that I let you go on and on about Ann because I am sick of hearing about it, so I apologize, okay?"

Obviously, this is an example of a statement that falls very short of a heartfelt apology. Mary is actually blaming John for her mistake. It is an example of emotional illiteracy that is worse than no apology at all.

7. Accepting the Apology. Again, the correct response to such a statement, as is the case with the response to an action/feeling statement, is to acknowledge the facts that are being stated.

Error F. Bashing the Righteous. John could use this opportunity to take out his anger and hurt feelings on Mary.

"Well, it's about time you apologize for patronizing me. I resent it, and I hate you for it."

This won't do. If John is angry or hurt, he can use

142

an action/feeling statement to deal with his reaction: "It makes me angry that you have let me go on and on about Ann when you didn't want to. I am also hurt. Thanks for the apology though."

The seven steps presented in this chapter will go a long way toward providing a positive emotional environment for emotions to be expressed, whether it be between friends, lovers, or co-workers or within a family. As people become skilled in the use of these techniques, they become second nature, and people lose their initial awkwardness. The techniques simply become part of everyday routine, similar to brushing one's teeth, raking the leaves, or walking the dog. Once assimilated, they contribute to a well-ordered life in which emotions are acknowledged and integrated into our lives.

CHAPTER 13

COMMITMENT, FRIENDSHIP, HONESTY, JEALOUSY, AND OTHER GRADUATE STUDIES

So far I have been speaking about the fundamentals of a well-ordered and effective emotional life. Let us now discuss some important emotional topics on a more advanced level.

Commitment

I have used the word *commitment* often in this book. It is a major concept in the relationships between men and women, and a subject of serious concern to most men.

Some men can't make commitments at all; others have made one and been burned, so they are afraid of getting hurt again. Some men think they are committed to someone and find that they are not. Some feel that they are not ready to "settle down" and are afraid of giving up their freedom.

When we can't commit ourselves to a specific person, it may be that we feel the person just isn't right. This fear, as I have remarked before, is especially strong in men for whom making a commitment usually means agreeing to provide food, clothing, housing, transportation, and all the material needs of a woman, plus an indeterminate number of children, for the rest of his life. In addition to all that, he is never to relate intimately to another woman again. Given the magnitude of the task, it makes sense that we would be afraid of making a mistake by choosing someone less than perfect.

Women aren't so frightened of making commitments because what is expected of them doesn't seem as onerous, though if the truth be known, it may be even more onerous in the long run.

Commitment to a primary, life-long, intimate relationship is more than anything an attitude. It is today's sincere intention to be wholly dedicated to a relationship. This does not, however, imply that having made a commitment, we have sealed our fate and never will, in fact, decide to leave it. Commitment, in other words, is not a ball and chain. It only means that we are giving it everything we have *now* and sincerely *intend* to continue to do so. Whether that commitment does, in fact, continue in the future depends on what happens. Commitment is necessary for a long-term, intimate relationship, but it is no guarantee of happiness and success, as we shall see.

"I love you unconditionally; I am with you without reservations, and I am not waiting for someone better to be with." That is the basic statement of commitment.

145

A lot of problems between men and women are really problems of commitment. Let us look at the relationship between Sara and Eric, who are in an intimate, sexual, long-term relationship; in other words, they are married. We assume, and they assume, that they are mutually committed. Eric, however, is listless in the relationship. His eye wanders. He is not affectionate with Sara but flirts with other women, which drives Sara insane with jealousy. He says he is not jealous, and he resents Sara for her jealousy and demands. One way to understand and analyze the situation is that Sara is possessive, and Eric is not, when what may actually be happening is that Sara is committed to Eric, but Eric is not committed to Sara. Commitment is the issue between Eric and Sara, more than any other consideration.

It's often difficult to assess whether one person is committed to another because people will lie about their commitments. The guilt associated with entering a serious intimate relationship while not really being committed is strong. Very few are willing to admit their true level of involvement. When commitment is weak, the amount of camouflage and mystification (read "lying") that goes on can be staggering.

Commitment cannot be engaged in without a reasonable level of trust, and trust is an elusive emotion. Some people are foolishly trusting and willing to commit themselves to someone whom they have known for a few days or even hours, with predictable disappointment. Others are so suspicious they can never really trust their partner and, therefore, never fully commit themselves.

People are justified not to trust easily or commit themselves without cold investigation and thought. Women have every reason to believe that men's interest in them

146

is motivated by an intense need for sexual and emotional nourishment, which, when provided, doesn't necessarily take them much further into commitment. Likewise, men justifiably fear that women's interest in them is as a provider of physical necessities or emotional support and that once a commitment is secured, nothing much can be expected in return. Both men and women reasonably fear being trapped into arrangements that threaten to be unsatisfactory or to exploit and bind them for the rest of their lives.

Consequently, the making of commitments is a process requiring and deserving careful attention to practical and emotional issues:

"After Katryn and I were lovers for about two years, it became obvious that we had to make some decisions. I would have been happy to continue as we were, but she was getting antsy. She wanted to know what she could count on. Otherwise, she wanted to move on. She was in love with me but wanted to have children. So it was time to fish or cut bait.

"I was terrified. First, I thought, 'Okay, Jack, just jump in,' so I tried that, but it was no good. She realized I was not into it. So I tried to pull out, but that didn't work either. I really loved her. So we talked about what it all meant. I told her my fears; being trapped, not being ever able to look at another woman. We talked about dishes, diapers, days out with the boys and the girls. It all seemed doable and we agreed to a lot of things and even wrote them down. I took the plunge, and eventually we got married. Getting married was easy once I agreed to go for broke. I am glad I did it, but I don't know if it would have worked without that period of discussion."

Relationship Contract

Katryn and Jack's example points out the need for exploring what the actual, everyday agreements in the relationship are going to be. Commitment is essential, but it is, as I have said, only an attitude; it does not deal with dishes, diapers, and yardwork. The old marriage agreement is only a contract by default. It doesn't say what should happen if Katryn decides to go back to work after the babies are born. It might turn out that when push comes to shove, the assumption was that he'd work, and she'd do housework. Today's relationships throw all those assumptions into question and require a fresh, hard look. For instance:

1. Who will do the cooking, the dishes, and the housework? If it is to be shared, who will do how much and when? Are the agreements made open for modification, and how?

2. If children are wanted, how will the decision to become pregnant be made? Who will feed, diaper, get up in the night? Who will do child care, drive the children to school, to the doctor, and so on? In what proportion?

3. How much time will be spent together? How many nights out will people have? Can friends, even intimate ones, have an emotional claim to either of the partners? Which friends? How much of a claim?

4. How much and what kind of sex do the partners expect from each other? How will they ask for it if they want it and decline if they don't? What will be the assumptions about other sexual partners? Total monogamy? Only on trips of more than 500 miles? Never with friends? Okay, but don't talk about it? Total honesty?

148

Marriage is supposed to signal commitment. In most cases, those who marry intend to make it last a lifetime. Yet, we know how many such commitments don't work. Many couples who don't marry are in fact more committed than some who do. Engagements, showers, and wedding ceremonies don't necessarily produce long-term committed relationships. Such committed relationships are the result, instead, of a much more complicated set of circumstances; trust, sexual and loving connections, compatibility, mutual self-interest, and workable agreements.

How to Be a Good Friend

When everything is said and done, a man who loves a woman should be a good friend to her. Friendship often precedes falling in love and eventual commitment. In fact, marriages between erstwhile friends, who eventually fall in love, have an exceptionally good chance of being successful because when they come out of the "in-love" fog, they will still know and like each other.

Consequently, knowing how to be a good friend is an important skill for a man. Being a good friend is a simple concept, but it is not always clear what a good friend is like, what he does and does not do.

The following are four rules of friendship, which I have found valid and useful. One can try to be a good friend even if no agreements, or even a clear, mutual relationship exists. But ideally a friendship is a conscious, cooperative relationship that involves both people equally. Whenever an acquaintance seems to be progressing in the direction of becoming a friend, it's worthwhile to formalize the process by making a contract that will be taken as seriously as the marriage

149

contract or any other contract between two people.

Here are the four rules:

1. We agree to participate equally in the friendship, to work equally hard to keep it alive, not to neglect it, and to be available when the other needs us.

2. We agree to be completely truthful with each other. (See honesty, below.)

3. We agree not to power play each other in order to get what we want; instead, we agree to ask for what we want, not to do anything we don't want to, and to negotiate toward a mutually satisfactory compromise.

4. We agree to spend a certain amount of time with each other and to let each other know when our commitment to the friendship weakens. If the amount of time spent with each other needs to be changed, we agree to give reasonable notice with nurturing and caring.

All friendships can benefit from faithful adherence to the first three points. Point four determines how extensive a friendship it will be. In a simple friendship the time spent together might be a few hours a month or week, while in a marriage all of the nights, most of the evenings, and a large proportion of the free time might be devoted to each other.

Two lovers may agree to spend two or three nights and evenings and one weekend a month together, but to reserve the other nights and days for themselves and other people.

In any case, agreements need to be made and followed or changed by mutual consent. When agreements are not clear but are assumed, the relationship may work only if, by lucky accident, what both people want is reasonably similar. But when that is not the case, difficulties will develop. Only trouble can result when two people enter into a relationship wanting different things but not discussing them while assuming they agree.

For instance, quite commonly people have different ideas about fidelity and monogamy. Consider the following example:

Several months after meeting and going out fairly steadily, Sarah discovers that Dan (who she knows is a terrible flirt) has started to go out with another woman. She's very upset, although she realizes that he never agreed to see her exclusively. He is annoyed and unsympathetic, and they find themselves in a major fight.

The problem is that they never discussed the nature of their new relationship. It turns out that Sarah assumed, because they were making love, that a monogamous agreement had been sealed between them. Dan never actually saw it that way. He did not assume such an agreement, but he never felt up to mentioning it. Now he realizes that he doesn't want the relationship to become that serious. His idea was that they were friends; her idea was that they had become exclusive lovers. Only if they discuss each other's expectations and willingness to fulfill them can the friendship survive.

Another important aspect of friendship is that it's often considered a second-class relationship when compared to exclusive intimate commitments. Consequently, it is assumed that a friendship will take a back seat when one of the two people gets more "seriously" involved. Discounting the importance of friendships with respect to so-called "primary" relationships is a mistake, in my opinion. Good friendships often last longer and can be just as valuable as, if not more so than, primary relationships. In any case, they are invaluable adjuncts to primary relationships, providing balance, relief, and support that add to the strength of committed relationships.

If a friendship is to be serious, it has to be given first-class status regardless of other developments in one's love life. I have found friends to be the source of all manner of benefits. In times of difficulty with my partner, friends have helped clarify what I was doing wrong, have given me moral support, have provided comic relief, have listened to my complaints without taking sides, or taken sides when needed, have taken my mind off my troubles, have taken me to the movies, and have let me sleep over. In happy times they have enriched my life with their presence and points of view, have cooked meals, done child care, gossiped, given me advice and asked for advice about their own troubles, gone on trips and celebrated life with me. But, this has been the case because I take my friendships as seriously as I take my committed relationships and would never relegate them to second place; nor would I accept being a friend to someone who would treat my friendship in that manner.

Honesty

Being truthful is, in my opinion, the only choice in a relationship that means to be long-lasting, intimate, and committed. Lies are the single most corrosive influence upon relationships—despite popular songs and half-baked advice about little white lies. Granted, the truth is sometimes hard to take. But the truth is less painful up front than when it comes out after months or years of accumulated, compounded lies. Truthfulness is the basis for trust; without it a relationship is like a house of cards, ready to collapse at the first revelation of dis-

152

honesty. When trust is destroyed in a relationship, what remains can only be a shadow of its former self.

Honesty obviously requires that no lies be told. But, as in the courtroom, complete honesty requires "the truth, the whole truth, and nothing but the truth." To tell the whole truth, lies of omission must also be avoided.

Regarding lies of omission, men have a tendency not to say whatever they think a woman won't like to hear, out of a false sense of gentlemanly courtesy. But women, especially today's women, don't have to be handled with kid gloves. They aren't victims needing to be rescued.

Talking straight is the opposite of lying by omission. Being truthful includes saying what one wants and how one feels. Asking for what one wants is especially important for men. Traditionally, men and women expected that she would know and give what he wanted without his having to ask. This expectation can be disastrous with a modern woman. She will wait until he asks; he will not ask and will sulk when she doesn't come across. Serious misunderstandings can start in that manner, and there is only one solution; men have to learn to ask for what they want.

Not keeping secrets also implies that people will be expected to be openly (though lovingly) critical. I know that this advice flies in the face of what we are taught about the relationships between the sexes. But women (and men) are a great deal sturdier than myth credits them. In the long run, modern women prefer to hear the truth. So men will be doing everyone a favor by saying even the hard things that they are scared to say or the things they won't say to preserve a sense of romance or to maintain control. A relationship based on honesty and truth is, without any question, stronger and more enjoyable than one riddled with evasions and half-truths.

People who argue against the value of complete honesty in relationships are often afraid of the cruelty that is possible under the guise of honesty. True, a cruel person can use honesty selfishly and insensitively, but my experience is that in the hands of such a person lies are even more hurtful than the truth, so that, in the end, honesty is best.

Jealousy

The rules of commitment appear to demand that we find everything we need in one person. The unrealistic expectations that we have of any one person fulfilling all of our needs are often responsible for the eventual breakdown of our commitments and ultimately the failure of relationships.

A modern woman is likely to have other interests than her partner. As has been the case with men, she may rub elbows and be friends with, perhaps even have intimate friendships with, other men. Men who are not accustomed to having that shoe on the other foot might find themselves faced with intense jealousy that will need to be managed.

"A possessive man," said one woman friend of mine, "is the ultimate drag. The moment I get the feeling a man is going to try and own me, I lose interest, completely. I don't care if he is dreamboat number one, rich, sensitive, whatever. I see a possessive man, and I run the other way as fast as I can. I want to be loved, not owned. I am not interested in having a bunch of different lovers, but I am even less interested in having a big squishy man hanging on me."

Jealousy, the green-eyed monster, is a much-feared, much-misunderstood emotion. Some believe, in this age of relaxed sexual mores, that jealousy is an unworthy emotion to be suppressed in an evolved human being. Some people claim not to be jealous, but discover that this is a theoretical proposition that falls apart when put to a serious test. Some are proud of their strong jealousy, which they believe to be evidence of their equally strong love.

There are, as far as I can tell, two major situations that provoke jealousy in people. One form of jealousy has to do with love and the other has to do with control.

Control Jealousy

When jealousy has to do with possessiveness, it is connected to primitive, territorial instincts that are applied to objects as well as people. The desire that some people have to define their property and to exercise control over it manifests itself with their sexual partners in the form of jealousy. In feeling this kind of jealousy, we don't consider the other person's emotional needs; we simply are unwilling to accept the loss of control over an object we own. We may not even love or care about the person. We may ourselves be involved with second, third, and fourth lovers, but we regard that person as "ours."

Our culture constantly reinforces the experience of jealousy in stories, movies, TV, magazine articles, humor, and especially songs. Being jealous is not generally considered a problem; in fact, it is thought to be a sign of how much we love the people we are jealous

155

of and how passionately we feel about losing them.

In fact, people who suffer control jealousy are profoundly affected by their need to possess and have power over another person whom they supposedly love. When seen in this light, it's difficult to regard jealousy as a positive emotion worthy of being associated with love. But it is often associated with love and then usually founded on the fear of loss, the terror of being alone—in short: insecurity and lack of confidence.

Deficit Jealousy

A second form of jealousy has to do with a sense of unfair exchange. When people enter into relationships with each other, they quite naturally offer each other love, nurturance, support, physical and material benefits, all without particularly discussing the terms of the exchange but assuming, or hoping, that the exchange will be a fair one. But fairness does not necessarily follow.

After the initial flurry of romantic excitement, things settle down to a pattern that is often anything but fair. Mary listens to everything John says while John tends to stare blankly when she speaks to him. When John is sick, Mary drops everything to take care of him, whereas when Mary is sick, John seems incapable of anything but the most cursory nourishing gestures. Mary constantly touches, caresses, and cuddles John, whereas John neither appreciates nor reciprocates these favors. If one is willing to look at the relationship as an exchange of a variety of needs, one might discover that Mary provides John with nurturing, home-cooked meals, housecleaning, and genital-sexual outlet, while John provides Mary with a paycheck, protection from physical attack, garden work, and sensual-sexual outlet. This

156

may be a crazy quilt of unacknowledged exchanges and needs, but it is an arrangement that somehow carries them both through their daily life together.

Now, let us say that John takes some of what is part of the exchange, withdraws it from the relationship and gives it to somebody else. At the office and after work hours, he now spends time with, smiles at, and nurtures Jane. Jealousy may reasonably ensue. This is not a matter of possessiveness, but a violation of an agreement of exchange, and it leaves Mary unfairly treated. The relationship between Mary and John is one in which a great deal of inequity already exists. Mary is giving John a lot of nurturing, in exchange for which she gets very little except a man to call her own. If John now proceeds to apply some of his stingily given affection to someone else, Mary may experience a tremendous amount of jealousy that has to do not so much with possessiveness as with an injured sense of fairness that is completely understandable.

Jealousy Management

The gut-wrenching feeling that jealousy can be and the anger and pain associated with it are for some people probably the closest that they come to extreme emotion. It is, accordingly, a good opportunity to practice the development of emotional literacy and the management of emotions. Management, in this sense, does not refer to the suppression or discounting of emotion but to recognizing, validating, and accounting for it.

Jealousy management requires the conviction that emotions are an important part of ourselves to be honored and considered. Yet we also need to remember that they can be destructive, operate against our better judgment, and cause us to do things we don't want to do. Jealousy management, when successful, has a side effect. It often leads to management of other emotions like anger, guilt, or shame, since jealousy management is merely part and parcel of the larger activity of emotional literacy. Dealing with jealousy requires that when we feel it, we speak of it. If jealousy threatens to overwhelm us, good emotional management requires that we control our impulses to accuse, attack, or make a scene, and that, instead, we determine its source.

When feeling jealousy, the first task is to determine whether it's control or deficit jealousy. In order to practice emotional literacy, it's important to be able to express early on, candidly and without guilt, the various circumstances in which jealousy is aroused. Talking about it, through action/feeling statements and paranoid fantasies, thinking about it, and making decisions about it will go a long way to dealing with it.

If it turns out that what we are feeling is control jealousy, we need to resolve to withdraw our support of it, to let it pass as we pledge ourselves to our partner's freedom of action. This is an effort of the will, a decision to live according to one's principles rather than at the mercy of one's emotions.

It is helpful here to tell oneself things like:

"I love her but she is not my property."

"If I really love her, I will trust her and stop trying to control her."

"Trying to control her will not make her love me or cause her to go along with me."

"If she goes along with me unwillingly, she becomes a slave."

"Her freedom (and mine) are more important than my desire to dominate."

When control jealousy is disposed of and kept out of a relationship, deficit jealousy remains an accurate index of how equitably the relationship is being conducted.

If it turns out that the jealousy we feel is deficit jealousy, we need to correct the inequities that cause our discomfort. When deficit jealousy occurs, agreements have to be made to change the situation so it becomes fair. Deficit jealousy must be acknowledged and dealt with by changing how people act with each other; it will not be chased away by the sort of act of will that I suggest for control jealousy.

Dealing with jealousy will be beneficial to the relationship and to our development as loving, responsible, and emotionally literate men. When control is relinquished and mutual commitment is backed up by generous give and take of affection, sexuality, nurturing, resources, and gifts, jealousy becomes unnecessary and irrelevant. A committed relationship free of jealousy is a crowning achievement of all that is nurturing, cooperative, and freedom-loving between people.

CHAPTER 14 | CONCLUSION

It has worried some men that as they give up their aggressiveness, their competition, their "macho" tendencies and become sweet and loving, they will also somehow lose their male *élan*.

Large numbers of men, however, are going through these changes. And as we become accustomed to our new, more pliable selves, we may be feeling somewhat empty. We may feel hollowed out, somehow, of something identifiably male that we can call our own.

Of the many wondrous things that human beings can do, only women can carry to term and breast-feed humankind; what equivalent miracle can men perform?

Vacillating between our former cold, soldierly selves and our newfound open hearts, we sometimes wonder whether becoming what women want is sufficient to fulfill our needs.

Undeniably, the new male context warrants some discussion. Over dinner one evening I asked my friend Jackson, "What *are* we going to do about this situation of women's obvious superiority, now that we have given up ours? How can we catch up?"

His answer, "We'll start knitting clubs."

Dumbfounded, I looked at him, trying to understand

what he meant. His lips were pursed in a smile. Then we both burst out laughing. I suddenly saw the glimmer of a simple answer.

As men who have given up their macho ways and are concentrating on pleasing women, we need also to please ourselves and each other. We need to find what our essence is, and we can do that only with other men, as we spend time together being exactly what we are, making no effort to live up to any expectations.

Released from the limiting male assumptions that have kept us competing with each other, afraid to appreciate and truly love each other, reluctant and reticent to trust and share, we may find that each other's male company is the next milestone in our development as human beings.

So when a man loves a woman and finally gives her what she wants, establishing once and for all that she is his equal, he may also find that he's suddenly open in a new way to finding his true identity in the company of men: fathers, sons, and brothers and friends to whom I lovingly dedicate this book.

BIBLIOGRAPHY

Ehrenreich, Barbara. *The Hearts of Men: American Dreams and the Flight from Commitment*. Garden City, N.Y.: Anchor Books, 1983.

Friedan, Betty. *The Feminine Mystique*. New York: W. W. Norton & Co., Inc., 1963.

Goldstein, Marc, and Michael Feldberg. *The Vasectomy Book*. Los Angeles: J. P. Tarcher Inc., 1982.

Hite, Shere. *The Hite Report: A Nationwide Study of Female Sexuality*. New York: Macmillan Publishing Co., Inc., 1976.

—————. *The Hite Report on Male Sexuality*. New York: Alfred A. Knopf, 1981.

Kerr, Carmen. *Sex for Women Who Want to Have Fun and Loving Relationships with Equals*. New York: Grove Press, Inc., 1977.

Morgenstern, Michael. *How to Make Love to a Woman*. New York: Ballantine Books, 1983.

Penney, Alexandra. *How to Make Love to a Man*. New York: Clarkson H. Potter, Inc., 1981.

Steiner, Claude. *The Other Side of Power*. New York: Grove Press, Inc., 1981.

—————. *Scripts People Live*. New York: Grove Press, Inc., 1974.